RULA

The castle in Dzików, where my forefathers danced, and where, had it not been for the Second World War, I would probably have been born and spent my early years.

RULA
MY COLOURFUL LIFE

RULA LENSKA

The Robson Press

First published in Great Britain in 2013 by
The Robson Press (an imprint of Biteback Publishing Ltd)
Westminster Tower
3 Albert Embankment
London SE1 7SP
Copyright © Rula Lenska 2013

Images of Rula Lenska and Dennis Waterman, pp. 94 and 118, reproduced by kind permission of Brian Aris (www.brianaris.com).

ISBN 978-1-84954-550-1

10 9 8 7 6 5 4 3 2 1

A CIP catalogue record for this book is available from the British Library.

Set in Caslon

Printed and bound in Great Britain by
CPI Group (UK) Ltd, Croydon CR0 4YY

To my wonderful mama and my precious daughter,

the two most special women in my life

Mama and Lalli.

CONTENTS

ACKNOWLEDGEMENTS

The hugest, warmest, heartfelt thanks to David Robson for his invaluable help, guidance, support and expertise on my journey.

To Jeremy Robson, my publisher, for his trust in me and for agreeing to take on this story, and to Tony Mulliken for leading me to him.

To my special daughter and my beloved siblings for their trust, love and support.

To dear Brian Deacon for always being there.

To my agent Paul Pearson for his care and enthusiasm.

To all my friends for their love and warmth … who have promised they will buy the book…

To Colin … my generous webmaster…

My christening, 1947.

CHAPTER 1

FAR FROM MY
GRANDFATHER'S CASTLE

I was born Róza Maria Laura Leopoldyna Lubienska on 30 September 1947 in an army camp in Huntingdonshire, the daughter of a Polish count and countess who were themselves the children of long lines of counts and countesses. But, as my mother used to say, in England a count counts for nothing.

They had arrived as penniless refugees the previous year, my father after a military career at the shoulder of Poland's wartime leader, my mother after a harrowing journey involving exile to Yugoslavia, arrest and two and a half years' slave labour in Ravensbrück, the German concentration camp. As a little girl I loved hearing stories about her childhood in a castle filled with servants and surrounded by vast estates. It made me wonder how very different my own life would have been had it not been for the war. Would I have met my future husband galloping through the forest or at some grand ball in one of my ancestors' castles? As it turned out, I met my first husband at drama school and my second in an episode of *Minder*.

There has always been a part of my make-up that is not English. The Polishness in my heart is very strong, and even though I didn't actually go to Poland until 1989, after the collapse of Communism, I was very conscious and proud of my heritage. In fact, when I first arrived in Warsaw I felt as though my soul were coming home, but I also realised fairly quickly that we émigré Poles were not quite the same as the Polish Poles who had weathered Communism at first hand.

As a girl I sort of hated it. I was born in England, I lived in England and I wanted to be like everybody else. I had English school during the week, Polish school on Saturday and church most Sundays. Apparently when I was about seven I said to my mother, 'It's just my luck to have been born a Pole and a Catholic … It ruins my whole weekend.'

My mother was one of the kindest, gentlest and least bitter people I have ever known, which considering the extraordinary hardships she endured is astounding. She and her siblings were all deeply affected by manic depression, inherited from their father. Throughout their lives they needed medication to stabilise their terrifying mood swings. Mama had to be hospitalised during the worst times, particularly after the birth of my youngest sister and brother.

My father was not very forthcoming about his early life. He joined the Polish diplomatic service as a young man and was personal secretary to Józef Beck, the Minister for Foreign Affairs. He left Poland before the war broke out, leaving behind his mother and his sister, who was a nun. He never quite forgave himself for having abandoned them. He felt particularly sad that he didn't get his mother out, though perhaps not so bad about his sister because she was already in a convent. I only met my father's mother a couple of times in England and a couple of times in Munich.

During the war he was adjutant to General Sikorski, the Polish Prime Minister in exile who died in a plane crash off Gibraltar in July 1943. In fact, my father was due to be on that plane but at the last moment Sikorski's daughter arrived and took his seat. He was one of the last people to see Sikorski alive and the first to go out on the boats when the plane crashed into the ocean. In 1944 he fought with General Anders and the second Polish corps at the Battle of Monte Cassino.

My mother and her family had escaped Poland when the Germans invaded in September 1939 and had gone to Yugoslavia. For two years they lived happily in Italian-controlled Croatia. She met an Italian officer, fell in love and got engaged. Then the Germans invaded and the Poles were handed over to them. Many, like my mother and grandmother, were sent off to concentration camps. When they emerged at the end of the war my mother wanted to make contact again and marry her fiancé but my grandmother forbade it: 'The Italians betrayed the Poles.' My mother hardly knew my father when they got married. The couple were brought together by his army friends in cahoots with her mother. Their wedding was in Rome. It was a dynastic marriage, more or less arranged, two people from aristocratic backgrounds, formed in a Poland that no longer existed. At the end of the war the Allies had handed the country over to the Russians, the Poles' historic enemies, condemning it to more than four decades of Communist rule. Throughout their lives my parents still believed they would one day be able to return to the country they loved.

My mother wrote in a memoir:

We arrived in England in November straight off the boat from sunny Italy to a thick yellow fog and it was very cold. My husband and I had booked into a little guesthouse in Kensington but he had to go to Paris. I was left alone. The fog was so thick I couldn't even see the other side of the street so I stayed indoors reading, living off cold milk and jam, constantly feeding the coin-operated gas and electricity meters. Spring came and we stayed.

In another entry she described how things felt a couple of years later:

We were really very poor but by now I had my first child and we were already a bit happier in England. I was learning to speak English and feeling a little less of a 'bloody foreigner'.

4

I was learning how to do all the basic jobs myself – cooking and laundry and caring for my child, none of which I had ever done in Poland. It was a hard life lesson. Sometimes I remember thinking guiltily that concentration camp had in some ways been easier because you were told what to do and how to do it. And despite the terror and the screaming and the twelve-hour work days and the beatings you were free inside. Here it seemed I was never free, I found being an ordinary housewife incredibly difficult at first. It helped being young because young people are malleable and find it easier to adapt to a life so completely different from how it was before. And one of the things I learned to love about England was its freedom for individual identity.

My father bought a house in Willesden Green in northwest London – 29 Teignmouth Road. By this time I had a little sister, Gabriella, always known as Gaba or Buna. The Poles have this strange habit of diminutising names in many different ways – though my real name is Róza Maria I have always been Rula, or Rulka or Rulina or Rulinder. My mother was Elizabeth but everyone called her Bisia or Beniek. And my father, christened Ludwik was, all 6ft 4in. of him, always known to everyone as Lulu.

When I was small, the house, rather large and on three floors, was almost always full of my mother's family. Her mother, who was very weak, lived on the first floor – I absolutely adored her and she me. She taught me to knit and crochet. In her youth she had been beautiful. Now she was a tiny, frail-looking woman, quite stern, who went to church daily if she was strong enough. We called her Baba or Babi, which is Polish for granny.

For some reason she was very tolerant with me but rather less so with my sister Gaba, who could be very naughty. On one occasion, Babi was in the bathroom washing her hair and Gaba sneaked into her room to nick a couple of the delicious treats which Babi used to hide in her cupboard. These were stuffed prunes covered in chocolate, which she gave to us on special occasions. Gaba had her mouth full when Babi walked in and said 'Gaba?' in a threatening tone and Gaba, aged nine or so, leapt out of the first-floor window to the lawn below. Thank God she didn't hurt herself. But she was so terrified of Babi.

My mother's youngest brother Arthur was also often there. A very colourful, larger-than-life character, he liked his drink and having a wild time. Both he and Jas, the older brother, were hellraisers and incredibly handsome in their day. In later years, when I was living with Dennis Waterman in our house in Buckinghamshire, the two brothers loved nothing more than spending an evening round the snooker table with flowing alcohol and very loud music – two members of my family that Dennis definitely enjoyed spending time with.

Also, Ciocia (aunt in Polish) Marys or Maryna, Mama's youngest sister, was sometimes with us before she got married. She was very beautiful and great fun and we are still incredibly close. When Mama died she became my sort of surrogate mother.

My parents mixed in predominantly high-class society, often at Ognisko, The Polish Hearth Club in Kensington, which was central to the social life of their group. Most of the men seemed to be my father's age, all ex-army, some of them in the secret service, some of them having fought for Britain in the Battle of Britain. They would sit around forever discussing the war and what had gone wrong.

The Polish Hearth was the place for weddings and funerals, concerts and all manner of special events, as well as sometimes for Sunday lunch. At Christmas and Easter there would be the breaking of the Host, and a glass of wine. Most of the ladies I met there were titled; I had to curtsy to them. Most of the gentlemen, incredibly well behaved and gallant, would kiss my hand even when I was a very young girl.

I was astounded sometimes at how many 'aunts and uncles' I had. Most of them weren't genuine aunts and uncles, of course, though a real great-uncle of mine was a prince. I took it all for granted. There were so many counts and countesses; they were just like Mr and Mrs. It was only when I got a little bit older that I thought, 'If they are a prince and princess, why aren't they stinking rich? Why haven't they got huge great castles and palaces and enormous estates? And if my parents are a count and countess, why aren't we rich?'

Although she had a very privileged start to life, arrogance was never a part of my mother's character. Her upbringing had been strict, with an emphasis on unselfishness, respect for her elders and a sense of duty, all things that she was determined to pass on to us, her children.

She used to talk about her childhood in Poland and the magical upbringing she had. She loved skating on ponds on the estate. Sometimes her father would pull the children on their skates behind the car across private lakes that seemed endless. And she remembered with delight going mushroom picking in the forest with the whole family, cousins and uncles and aunts, and of course the retinue of servants that used to go with them.

She would tell me about the woodmen who rescued baby animals – owls, foxes and even once a bear cub – and about the conservatory attached to my grandfather's house, which grew the most stunning exotic fruit. They had white peaches and when we used to see ordinary yellow peaches in the local shops here she would say, 'Ah, they never smell as good as the ones we had in Poland.' They even grew pineapples. And though my mother was the grandchild of the owner of the estate, it was still much more fun stealing the fruit from the conservatory than eating it when it was placed on the table. She wrote:

My grandparents' castle where I spent much of my childhood had been the seat of my family for centuries. The surrounding estates were enormous, like a self-sufficient country within a country. There were horses and dogs and hunts and the house was always full of family and guests. There were people who had worked for my forefathers for centuries. All around for miles and miles were farms and forests and carp lakes and hospitals and factories and schools and vodka distilleries and sawmills that my ancestors had built for and with the people.

The Tarnowski family crest was emblazoned everywhere. Inscribed over the main door were the words of a sixteenth-century Polish poet, 'Lord, let us live in this family nest blessed with good health and a clean conscience', and from those words sprang a feeling of what seemed like eternal security, as if nothing could ever interrupt this harmonious life.

Christmas, Easter and name days, which in Poland are more important than birthdays, hold very special memories for me. At home in Willesden they were all imbued with strong Polish traditions that my sisters, brother and I, and all my cousins, still observe. Christmas in particular was magical. The tree would never go up until the day before Christmas Eve and the room was out of bounds.

This was a lovely echo of my mother's memory of Christmas in the Tarnowski castle, where a manservant would arrange delivery of a tree fresh from the forest and my grandmother would cover it with candles, red apples and icicles made of beet sugar from the factory down the road. The room would be filled with presents and the local boys would put on a puppet show in a candlelit box made with coloured paper to look like stained glass. 'They would tell stories about Death chasing Herod with his scythe,' my mother recalled. 'We would listen frightened and enthralled. They sang Latin and Polish verse and their puppet would collect money from us in its little sack. We gave the boys tea and cakes and begged them to come back again the following day.'

In my mother's house in Willesden the table was beautifully set, with a snowy-white tablecloth and all the best heirloom china we had, gleaming crystal glasses and red candles. Before the meal we would break the Host (*oplatek* in Polish), which we would share, wishing each other peace and health and happiness.

Then we would be led into the living room, where the tree glimmered with real candles. We each had a little pile of presents under the tree, but first we had to sing Polish carols in harmony until both parents were crying. That did not take long!

Before we were allowed to get to the presents, St Nicholas had to come. Dressed like a bishop in a long gown with a mitre, he was the European version of Santa Claus. This, of course, was my father, but it did not click for many years. The doorbell would go. An elegant, serious man would be led in and we would have to sit on his lap and he would ask us whether we had been good and honest children. Then he would give us a little sprig of birch and a tangerine, and only then could we get to our presents. What finally gave St Nicholas away as my father were his wedding ring and his shoes. And when I questioned my mother about it she made me promise not to tell my sister.

General Anders, the leader of the Polish government in exile, and his wife Irena were frequent visitors to my parents' house in north London. She had been a musical star in Poland before the war, with the stage name Renata, and carried on her career here in the Polish theatre where I started to tread the boards in my late teens. They used to come to play bridge. In those days, because most of my mother's family lived with us, my sister and I slept in adjacent cots in the sitting room, and my mother told me that often during the evening these little tousled heads would pop over the top of the cot bars to observe them playing.

Irena, the General's wife, was incredibly glamorous and always beautifully dressed, coiffed and perfumed. She also always had fingers well adorned with fabulous rings. To me she was like a fairy-tale queen.

Apparently, on my fourth birthday, at a rather grown-up tea party at our house she took me on her knee. She was wearing a fur stole, as was the fashion in those days, and she cuddled me close, calling me her *zlota kula*, which means 'golden ball', because my hair was a mass of ginger curls. 'What would you like for your birthday, a beautiful pink pram, a dolly that cries, or a little bicycle? Or maybe some lovely books? Tell me, I will give you anything you want,' she whispered.

I pointed to the biggest solitaire diamond on her hand and said, 'I want that, please.' Needless to say I didn't get it. Years later when I was taking part in a concert for her ninetieth birthday, I reminded her of this incident. We laughed so much.

At home the lingua franca was Polish, though both my parents had a good command of English. But my mother did make the most wonderful malapropisms. Years later when I told her that Dennis and I were going to get married she said, 'Darlink, you are going straight out of the frying pan into the Serpentine.' And on another occasion she introduced him to one of her American friends with 'This is my daughter's fiasco.'

CHAPTER 2

A WAR DANCE IN MY KNICKERS

My mother was having an incredibly tough time. There were two children – my sister and me – and a couple of dogs. There were of course no washing machines, no dishwashers, none of what we take for granted nowadays. I was about three and my sister Gaba was just under two. Ten minutes' walk from our house in Teignmouth Road was Walm Lane, where the shops were: small groceries, the chemist and the butcher, and the post office right near Willesden Green station. So it was my sister in her pram and me holding on to the pram and a little golden cocker spaniel called Jackie. We'd go off to the shops and in those days you could park the pram outside and go in and do your shopping and not worry about a thing.

On one occasion, Mama arrived back home with me and the dog and loads of shopping and she got into the house and said, 'I'm sure I've forgotten something,' and then – this was about half an hour after the event – 'Oh my God! Gaba in the pram.' She'd left her outside Graham the chemist's, so we rushed back there and she was happily sitting in her pram cooing, with people talking to her. Nowadays the child would probably have disappeared, or if not the child, the pram. I'm sure there were several occasions like that.

Mama always seemed warm, always smiling, always ready to talk, always happy to answer questions. She was a truly wonderful mother but her depressions could be very deep and painful. When things were very bad and she had to go into hospital, my sister and I were so little we didn't understand all that. We were just told she had to go away for a while.

I was expected to be a good example to my younger sister even when I was a small child. I was pretty cute, precocious and rather a show-off but loved by everybody and always ready to do my little turn, reciting Polish poetry or singing a little Polish song at the drop of a hat.

Letters to my mother always arrived addressed to Countess Lubienska; letters to my father were to Count Lubienski. Once when I asked my mother what these titles meant – I think she was in a hurry – she said: 'It's something like being king and queen but not quite.' In this country it had no meaning whatsoever, but in the Polish community it meant a lot.

My first school was the Jesus and Mary Convent, a cosy little place a short bus ride away from home. Already I was quite a tearaway and often in trouble, always a bit of a ringleader. In my first nativity play at school I was cast as a cockerel. Standing on a tall gym stool on one leg as the curtain went up,

I had to crow to announce the arrival of Angel Gabriel. I took this role very seriously. I had a beautiful costume with green tights and a feathered paper headdress. The curtain rose and I started crowing for all I was worth, but I had forgotten to go to the loo beforehand and suddenly, with all the emotion and the difficulty of holding the position on one leg, I wet myself. My mother said I was crying but still crowing, and I never let my leg drop till the curtain went down. Ever the pro!

My mother used to pick me up from school in the early days and she was always very friendly and was loved by my school chums. Most of them were Polish. One day they didn't run up to her and greet her as they usually did but seemed to shy away. When she asked me why, I said, 'Because I told them you and Papa were King and Queen of Poland.'

Ours wasn't a life of grandeur but it was pretty good, except that it seemed to be much stricter than all my friends'. They were allowed to go out, they went to people's houses during the week – we were only allowed to do that at weekends (if we had time after all our Polish duties). Instead of going out we played a lot of board games, which we loved. In fact, we sisters and our children play them to this day.

We had no television at home; I was sixteen by the time we owned one. Our reading was fairly censored. We had English homework and Polish homework too. The Polish Saturday school wasn't just language and traditional singing and dancing, it was a full curriculum – Polish history and geography and literature – pretty hard work for a young kid. And it was the rule that even though we went to an English school, in the house we had to speak only Polish.

Since both my parents arrived in England stateless, my father found it very difficult to get a decent job here. Eventually he went to work for the Polish–American Immigration Relief Committee based in Munich, looking after the thousands of displaced refugees from behind the Iron Curtain. So my mother was bringing us up by herself. Later he joined Radio Free Europe, also in Munich. Both of these were American-controlled so he ended up with an American passport – dual nationality, Polish and American. When he went away, he sort of put my mother in the care of Nicholas Carroll, an English journalist who was diplomatic correspondent of the *Sunday Times*. He and his wife, who was Polish, were close friends of my parents. They had two children, Nick and Iza, and we used to see them quite a lot as a family when we were very young. I certainly don't think my father intended things to turn out as they did.

When I was nine my gorgeous second sister was born. She was named Anna but mostly called Annula by the family. She was another redhead like me. So now there were three girls. It must have been really hard for my mother all alone. Except she was not quite alone. We always had Polish lodgers, young girls who would help out with babysitting and suchlike. With my father working and mostly living in Munich it was not much of a marriage and, somewhat inevitably, my mother fell passionately in love with Nicholas Carroll. I found out earlier than most people and I was horrified. I didn't understand. Why would I? I was just a young girl, not yet at secondary school.

This liaison was conducted in secret for many years. I knew long before my sister Gaba and it was very hard not to share it. I was very distressed by it because at that young age my father was still a god to me. My sister Anna was very small and the effort of looking after her, combined with the affair and her generally weak state, threw my mother into a very bad depression.

That year I moved on to Sacred Heart, a Catholic grammar school in Hammersmith. This was a big, serious institution, a world away from my primary school, though they did have nuns in common. I lasted only about two years there. I was far too rebellious. I was expelled. My mortal sins were doing a war dance on the school roof wearing my gym knickers and swinging a lacrosse stick and, to make matters worse, getting caught doing somersaults on the train in school uniform while eating pickled cucumbers.

My family were distraught. They thought I had brought shame on them. Things were in turmoil anyway. My mother was in a bad way and she was in love but still trying to pretend she wasn't. When her affair with Nicky became public she was cruelly ostracised by the older members of the Polish community, particularly the titled ones.

Then, on top of everything, she found out she was carrying Nicky's child, at the age of forty-three – very late in life in those days. This led to a full-blown nervous breakdown. Little Anna spent nearly a year in a sort of convent in Virginia Water for children who were having problems at home.

When my mother found out that she was pregnant she went to Munich to tell my father. They were still married. He was a most honourable, gentle man and he said he would bring the child up as his own and it could carry his name and there was no need for any scandal. But she and Nicky wanted to be together. So my father agreed, not immediately there and then, but he accepted there would have to be a parting of the ways. In the Catholic religion divorce is a mortal sin and my mother was deeply devout. But she did get divorced and soon after their son Andrew was born she and Nicky were married.

By then I had been sent away to boarding school – the Ursuline Convent at Westgate-on-Sea in Kent. I went at thirteen. Part of me thought 'Oh, Enid Blyton, *Malory Towers*, *Famous Five* – it will be like that.' I was excited to get away from home because I felt rather cooped up. I was still very much under my mother's thumb and was expected to be well behaved. So there was the thrill of the unknown, which delighted me. On the other hand there was also the strong feeling I was being sent away because of circumstances beyond my control, and the hurt of knowing my parents were going to be separating and that my mother would have this new husband who would become my stepfather.

I didn't understand how my mother could leave my father. I didn't know that my parents had never been a love match, that it had been an arranged marriage. To me they had always seemed incredibly close and as it turned out, despite every-thing, they did remain best of friends for the rest of their lives.

At boarding school I found a lot of fun and friendship and my sister Gaba joined me there a year later. But if I thought things were going to be free and easy I should have known better. I had already had quite a lot of experience with nuns. I ought to have guessed life would be strict as it had been at both my London convents. Even when we were tiny girls at primary school we had to curtsy to the nuns in the corridor.

It was quite something preparing for boarding school: every bit of clothing had to be name-tagged. The uniform was dark green pleated skirts with green-and-white striped blouses and a tie with a gold motif, and a green cardigan in the winter, with a green velvet hat and knee-high fawn-coloured socks and sensible shoes. When I arrived there, because my birthday is in September I was put in with the fourteen-year-olds.

I unpacked in a dormitory of twelve people in curtained-off cubicles. I had been used to a room with just my sister but I immediately became part of a group led by a girl called Veronica Tweed, who to this day remains one of my closest friends. And I remember one of the first things she said to me was, 'Have you got any handsome brothers or cousins?' I'll never forget that!

My hair was pretty long and the rule was that it had to be in a plait or a ponytail or whatever, but it wasn't supposed to touch your shoulders or your collar. I'd always been used to my mother plaiting my hair. Now I had to do my own. I did it in plaits or bunches or tied it up in a ponytail.

The nuns were in the full Darth Vader outfits, so you couldn't see most of their eyebrows, really, just the eyes – even the chin was covered. So it was the eyes, the nose and the mouth; long black robes to the ground; the high white wimple and a long black veil; and then a tabard over the top of that; a hanging cross and a rosary around the waist. And if you met a nun, any nun, whether it was the headmistress or one of the teachers or one of the nuns who worked in the reception area or in the refectory, even if you were running at a hundred miles an hour, you had to do a deep curtsy, which wasn't easy because the floors were highly polished red quarry tiles and very slippery.

In the dormitory everyone had their own very narrow single iron bedstead, a little stand with a bowl on top of it and a jug, and a tiny cupboard where you kept all your bits and pieces. There were two bathrooms (I don't think there were any showers) and you were allowed a bath once a week. My mother told me that when she went to boarding school a nun walked in when she was having a bath, and said, 'Why aren't you wearing a drape? You can see your own body.' And my mother said, 'Yes, I'm washing it,' and the nun said, 'On the chair there is a drape which you are supposed to put around your neck and drape over the side of the bath so you can't see your body when you're washing it.'

We didn't have any of that, but in the mornings we used to have to go and collect cold water – queue up for it, pour it into our jug and wash in it. Then the bell went, a loud clanging that sounded up and down the corridor at 7.30 a.m. Mass was at 8 a.m., so you had half an hour to wash, do your hair, line up and get ready to go down. And we had to go to Mass every day, apart from one day a week when we had an extra half-hour lie-in, which was the greatest of luxuries.

After the first two or three weeks, when the novelty had worn off, I became desperately homesick and used to cry myself to sleep in my little bed. Some nuns were kinder than others, but for the most part there wasn't a lot of physical contact and I was used to a very loving and affectionate mother. Our house was always full of hugs and cuddles. Still to this day I'm a very tactile person; so is my daughter with her child. All my siblings are always hugging and kissing each other – boys and girls. So that lack of contact was tough.

The lessons were tough too. I didn't last long in the class I was first put into. They were all nearly a year ahead of me and I was struggling, so I was put back a year and I was sad to be taken away from those new slightly older girls whom I was already looking up to.

First thing in the morning we used to assemble in the hall, a vast room with an enormous stage. The headmistress addressed us, then we would sing a couple of hymns and go off to our classes. One of the most memorable assemblies was in November 1963 when she told us President Kennedy had been killed. Mass hysteria. There were quite a lot of girls from Jamaica and Grenada who seemed particularly upset. And besides being a President and a hero, he was of course also a Catholic.

In the evenings the desks were all put out in the hall and we would sit there with one of the nuns on duty, in total silence, doing our homework for two hours or so. It was a long day. Then there would be a bit of playtime before it was teatime, and then bedtime.

Once a week we had to write home. I wrote to various other people too but home was obligatory. My father demanded we write to him in Polish and then when he answered he would send our letters back underlining all our grammatical mistakes in red pencil, which I thought was a bit cruel, but I am grateful now.

Then my little brother Andrew – Nicky's son – was born, and because my mother was in such a terrible state at the time, she actually couldn't cope with him for the first seven or eight months of his life and he had a sort of foster carer. So in the first two years we didn't see Mama that often when we had exeats from school because she was just not up to it. She was suffering terribly from the criticisms and cruelty some of the older members of the family and the senior members of the Polish community threw at her. My parents had been a very well-known couple and they were both much loved so it was regarded as a great scandal.

My stepfather Nicky bought a little old country cottage in Ash near Canterbury. From then on we used to go there when we had exeats. There was no electricity; we had to light gas lamps at night, and there was this old-fashioned metal hip bath. It was all rather romantic and hippy in the early days. I loved it. And there was a huge quarry behind, where we used to play rather dangerous games of sliding down. It was a very sporty, outdoorsy-type life.

Nicky was a keen boatsman. He had his own inflatable dinghy and he was a very accomplished rifle shot so I learnt, from quite an early age, to shoot at tins and at eggshells, which I think stood me in fairly good stead later on when I started playing snooker. He really tried to be a very good father substitute but I found it hard to warm to him. I adored and worshipped my father. So the relationship between my stepfather and me was a little bit guarded at first. But now, thinking back on those times, once we'd come to terms with the fact that Nicky was now our stepfather, we did have wonderful family times down in Ash.

I was delighted my mother was recovering and I was absolutely thrilled to have my baby sister back, and even more thrilled to have a new baby in the family, my little brother. Nicky was highly intelligent, very well travelled, spoke excellent Polish because of his first Polish wife, and he was very loving with my mother. He was also fairly firm with us but in a slightly different way from my parents. For instance, he was a great lover of music. He played the guitar and the clarinet very well and loved listening to opera, and he hated it when we put our pop records on his turntable. He used to tell us it ruined the stylus because the pop records were worse quality than operas and classical music. I soon got used to the idea of Mummy and Nicky.

For all the big holidays my sister and I travelled out to Munich to be with my father. We would get the train from London to Harwich, then the boat from Harwich to the Hook of Holland, then the train to Munich. This was from the age of about fourteen or fifteen. So for us, fairly green and immature, it was a huge adventure – just the two of us – and I always had to be in charge of my sister.

My father lived in a small bachelor flat in Munich. He had a huge circle of predominantly Polish friends, although there were quite a lot of Germans as well. The social life at Radio Free Europe was hectic, and he loved nothing better than going out with his teenage daughters. He was a flirt, but a harmless flirt. He loved his drink. Coming in for meals at the station or going out with him in the evening to visit his friends, or occasionally going to the theatre or the cinema, was great fun.

As for schoolwork, English Literature was always my favourite subject, particularly when we got on to Chaucer and Shakespeare. My English teacher was called Mother Mary of the Incarnation. I guess she was pretty young then, probably in her mid-twenties, but it was impossible to gauge the age of the nuns because you could see so little of them, which certainly made them look formidable. I seem to remember most of them wore glasses as well. I never really thought of the nuns as women; I regarded them as a breed apart. For a time I thought they might be on roller skates. They didn't seem to walk, they seemed to glide. I found most of them quite frightening but Mother Mary of the Incarnation was a huge support to me right from the very beginning.

So was Mother Bernadette, who taught French. Because I already spoke fluent Polish, other languages came very easily to me – I always used to get praise from her in the classes and I was always the first one to learn French songs and speak French poetry with a good accent, and I was good at my written work. So I liked her and she liked me. But though she was tiny, she was still scary.

Then there was Mother Mildred, who used to work in the reception and run the tuck shop on Saturdays. She had Parkinson's so her head was constantly shaking and we used to make terribly cruel fun of her, but she was adorable. Mother Veronica, who taught us science, had the most enormous buck teeth and she used to whistle and spit, so we used to try and get her to say words like 'photosynthesis', and then pretend that we were all being showered by her spitting.

I never did physics and chemistry, only biology. I did languages, history, geography – I think twelve O levels in all. And around that time there was a lay teacher called Mrs Boyd who started to come to do what might loosely be called drama classes. An older lady, she and I absolutely adored each other. I stayed friends with her right until her death. She came to see me in the theatre many times and when she died she left me all her small leather-bound editions of Shakespeare.

She and Mother Mary of the Incarnation became my steadfast mentors. When I was a junior the only plays were nativity plays and I was cast in good parts – Angel Gabriel first and then Joseph. I was often cast as a man. And then we did a play called *The Common Man*, quite a tough piece of theatre. I was given the lead role.

At the age of sixteen I applied for the National Youth Theatre. I didn't get in. At about the same time, my stepfather's mother died and left a huge trunk full of beautiful vintage tea dresses and long gowns. Now I look back with horror at how we cut up and adapted those vintage creations to fit the productions I was involved in – sacrilege! Apart from anything else, if I still had them I could have made a fortune on eBay.

We started a drama club in the school, the first time they had ever had anything like that. At the age of sixteen or seventeen I was allowed to produce and direct my first play – *Emma* by Jane Austen. Veronica, my great friend, played the title role and my sister never forgave me for casting her as a man.

By then I was allowed into the outside world a bit and when we were visiting my father in Munich there were a couple of young gentlemen who took an interest in me; one was Hungarian, Peter Zaboyi. I used to sneak off from my father's flat and come back in the early hours of the morning. I was still fairly innocent, and my father was never any the wiser. Even if he had been he was very relaxed and easy about giving us our freedom in certain ways.

He also used to send us off for skiing holidays. We didn't speak very good German, and I never liked the language, even though I did it for A level at school. I found it harsh and grating and ugly compared with Polish and French. We were dispatched to Austria with a group of people for an intensive four- or five-day skiing course. I was never much of a sports-woman but my sister Gaba was excellent. Of course there were boys in the group and a lot of flirting going on and we had so-called boyfriends.

We were staying in a sort of youth hostel and in the evenings after the skiing had finished we all got together and the boys thought it would be great fun to teach us some traditional German songs. When we got home my sister and I proudly launched into singing them. My father went purple – they were all Hitler Youth songs. The boys knew perfectly well what they were doing and they just thought it would be a bit of fun. They would have been delighted with their success if they'd known.

In the Christmas holidays, when I wasn't going to Munich I got involved in the Polish theatre at The Polish Hearth Club. We had Marian Hemar, one of Poland's best-known pre-war writers, poets and theatre directors, General Anders's wife Renata Bogdanska and four other amazing Polish divas, Lola Kitaiewicz, Irena Delmar, Marysa Drue and Wlada Majewska. I started off dressing them backstage in a tiny little space no bigger than a toilet, with five chairs. Frequently there were period costumes so I used to look after the wigs, the make-up and the hairdressing and dress these wonderfully exotic, glamorous women. I became very, very friendly with them and we stayed friendly until the end of their lives. Then I finally got two or three decent parts in Polish, and ever since I have had hopes of working in Polish theatre in Poland, or in Polish television, in Polish.

My dream then, of course, was to go straight from the convent to drama school. My parents were not at all happy about my desire to be an actress. Both of them thought it wasn't a dignified enough profession for somebody of my background. My father viewed it as a bit like being a prostitute. He desperately wanted me to go into something like the United Nations and use my languages.

At the end of each school year there was a prize day and some important person – often a bishop – would come to do the final honours. But in the year I finished my A levels they invited one of the country's favourite actors, Jack Warner, the benign, bike-riding, 'evening, all' Police Constable Dixon from *Dixon of Dock Green*, amongst the most loved television series ever. For me it was a huge thrill. I had secret hopes that maybe he might help me in some way. When he came to the school I was put in charge of looking after him because I was President of the Drama Club. Of course, I did everything I could to ingratiate myself with him and he was an absolute delight. We exchanged addresses and he said he would try to do what he could, and in fact, through him I got my first ever walk-on television part, as a policewoman in *Dixon of Dock Green* – non-speaking. I was about eighteen.

Wild days in Sardinia, 1969.

CHAPTER 3

FROM MY PRISON CELL

I worked for about nine months for Heinz 57 Varieties in Harlesden as a secretary to a retail manager – fairly boring, I must say. The only plus was that we were allowed, once a week, to raid the Heinz cupboard and take home as many tins as we wanted. But there was a problem – none of the tins had wrappers on, so you didn't know what you were getting. It could be Heinz tomato soup or it could be Heinz baked beans or it could be spaghetti hoops. It could be baby food, which was handy for various neighbours on Teignmouth Road – I was still living with my mother and the family. I also had a bit of a crush on my manager.

It was a traditional nine-to-five job, sitting typing, doing spreadsheets and taking shorthand. These, of course, were the days long before computers. I was by myself in an anteroom outside the retail manager's office. I very quickly realised that I was not cut out for a daily routine job. You know, come in, take a bit of shorthand, write the letters, get them signed, do a bit of filing, fetch teas and coffees, lunch in the canteen – and in Harlesden, not the most inspiring of areas.

I was doing it to please my parents, to somehow acquire this 'second string to my fiddle', as my mother put it, and to hone the secretarial skills I'd spent a year at Pitman's acquiring. I was a pretty good typist and I was OK at shorthand but there was no use for brain or imagination. I did go out a couple of times with my boss, but it didn't develop into a romance.

I also acquired my first car, bought from one of the chaps who worked at Heinz. I was told it was an ex-police car. It was an Austin, a real old banger with a running board and what they told me were bullet holes. I believed them. I went through a period of either feigning or being genuinely interested in the workings of a car. Because this car was falling to pieces I used to spend Saturday afternoons in grubby dungarees underneath it trying to mend the exhaust, which was making a dreadful noise. I was a tomboy and I thought it was rather kooky and funky to pretend I knew about how to sort out a car's problems, which I didn't really.

I used to skive off with Dadina, a girl who lived across the road and remains a close friend. I was having driving lessons, hadn't got my licence, but we got in my car and went off at dead of night. I was driving quite carefully down Kilburn High Road and suddenly a young cop stepped out in front of the car and flagged me down. I said to Dadina, 'Oh God, now we're for it, you'd better flutter your eyelashes and show as much leg as possible because the car is uninsured and I've got no road tax and I don't have a driving licence.'

So he taps on the window and I wind it down. He was a very good-looking policeman, not unlike a young Anthony Perkins. He said, 'Good evening, madam,' and I hitched my skirt a little bit higher up my thighs, and I said, 'Why did you stop us, Officer?' and he said, 'Because you didn't have your lights on,' and I said, 'Oh, I'm terribly sorry,' and I turned the lights on. Then he said, 'May I see your driving licence?', so I looked at him and fluttered my eyelashes and said, 'I'm afraid I haven't got one.'

'Insurance?'

'No.'

'Road tax?'

'No.'

'Is this car yours?'

'Yes, I've just bought it.'

He said, 'You know I could throw the book at you for this?'

I said, 'Yes, I'm well aware of that, Officer. I'm really terribly sorry.'

And then he said to me, 'Why don't you drive round the corner into Quex Road and I'll see you there with my colleague.'

For a moment I thought of doing a bunk but decided that wasn't a terribly good idea, so we drove round the corner and there's another very good-looking young policeman. It was a cold night and they had a little chat between themselves and the first one says to me, 'Look, how far away do you live?' So I said, 'Oh, about five minutes, between Kilburn and Willesden Green.' He said, 'I'll tell you what, if we can come back for a cup of coffee or a cup of tea, we'll forget all about it.'

So they jumped into the back of the car and I drove them home. Even when I was that age my mother was quite strict. I was always supposed to tell her what time I was coming in at night but my sister and I lived in an annexe next to the house with its own outside door so actually we could sneak in and out without anybody knowing. We and our policemen snuck into the bed-sitting room and had a cup of coffee and we remained friends. I picked them up off their beat quite a few times. There was no romance, just a friendship and a laugh.

After Heinz I got six months' work at a bank in the City. I honestly cannot remember what I did there. I think there were Bills of Lading or something, but what I remember most of all was the commuting from Willesden Green to the City and being just bored to tears.

I had promised my parents I would work for at least a year, and I had done it. Nothing was going to put me off applying to drama school. I was coming up to twenty and I said, 'OK, I've done what you asked me to do.' I had no desire to pursue my father's ambitions for me at the United Nations. True, I did speak several languages and I would learn another one – Italian – in extraordinary circumstances the following summer, but they certainly wouldn't be allowed to stand in the way of what I'd always dreamed of.

So far I had done everything that they had demanded. I had finished school, I had done my A levels, I had studied at Pitman's, I was a qualified secretary and I had worked for a year. 'Now,' I said, 'I am going to do my own thing.' And they said, 'Yes, great, but we can't afford to pay for drama school.' They were three-year diploma courses which were indeed extortionately expensive.

I applied for the Webber Douglas Academy and for the Central School of Speech and Drama. Webber Douglas was in Kensington and Central was in Swiss Cottage. I got invited for my two auditions, which involved a contemporary piece, a classical piece and a couple of pieces of improvisation on the day.

Despite their reservations my parents were quite supportive. They listened to me practising my pieces and I also did them for Anthony Quayle, the distinguished actor who had been a close friend of my father's since wartime days in Gibraltar when they were both aides-de-camp – my father to General Sikorski, Quayle to the Governor. He became a sort of mentor to me.

My classical piece was Titania from *A Midsummer's Night Dream* (a role I later played professionally at the open-air theatre in Regent's Park), and I can't remember the contemporary one. Anyway, I thought the audition pieces went pretty well.

When it came to the improvisations I was expecting hugely emotional scenes about coming home and admitting to your parents that you were pregnant or telling them that you'd killed somebody, but at Webber Douglas first I was told to be a fried egg and for the second improvisation I had to pretend to push a peanut up a hill with my nose. I didn't get into Central, which was my first choice, but I did get into Webber Douglas and I was awarded a bursary, which helped with finances.

The auditions were in late spring and the college year began in September. In between, as it turned out, I had an adventure and ordeal I would never forget, one I feared would put my whole dream in jeopardy – or even put an end to it.

The previous summer – the summer of '68 – I was twenty years old and had been offered a fun job by some enterprising young Italian gentlemen via my father of all people. They had told him they were setting up entertainment and nannying services in a very classy luxury hotel called Cala di Volpe on the glorious island of Sardinia. My father had mentioned that I was hoping to go to drama school and wanted to be an actress and that I had in fact done a bit of singing with my sister on Radio Free Europe light entertainment programmes – my uncle, younger brother of Mama, was the light entertainments director there. We were 'The Beat Girls', broadcast across the Iron Curtain into Poland with some success at the tender ages of sixteen and seventeen – my first taste of stardom!

My job would last over the summer months. There would

be no pay as such but I would have luxury accommodation
– so I was told – in this glamorous hotel, and three nights a
week I would sing a few numbers in the little nightclub bar in
the basement of the hotel with its resident band.

I was a fairly naive twenty-year-old but a bit of a rebel, and
headstrong, determined to go to drama school and become a
successful actress. I was a flamboyant hippy with a fairly outrageous taste in clothes and make-up and a definite penchant
for adventure and danger.

I was desperately excited about the Sardinia job and thought
I had really hit on a wonderful opportunity not only to play at
being a chanteuse and performer but to have an exotic, glamorous holiday with very little responsibility and for the first
time be truly on my own, on a sexy island peopled by the rich,
the exotic and the famous.

The first warning bells sounded as soon as I arrived, but in
those days I did not listen to warning bells. Actually, throughout
my life warning bells have either gone unheeded or prompted
me to rush towards them as if they were an invitation. The
hotel was on a beautiful white beach but I quickly found out
that instead of the single bedroom I had been promised I was
supposed to be sharing a four-bedded dorm with three young
Swedish girls hired as beach nannies for well-to-do families
who wanted their children entertained during the day and
babysat by night.

All went well for a while, until one of the girls started

having an affair with the entertainment manager of the hotel and complained how unfair it was that they had to do so much more work than I did for the same deal. To cut a long story short, the manager asked – demanded, actually – that I make myself available for the nannying jobs too, and that on the evenings when I was not performing I should be in the club bar persuading clients to buy champagne like the other girls, a sort of harmless hostess duty. I declined. It all got a little nasty and they told me that if I didn't agree to the extra duties I would lose my accommodation and my return ticket home after the holidays.

I told them they could stuff their job and their accommodation, I would find other work. By this time I was sweet on a young Italian student called Gianni Bussu, one of identical twins. Through him I found a job as a cashier and boutique attendant in a fashionable and famous club in Porto Cervo called Pedro's.

The restaurant was very swish and exclusive, the club and bar were full of international glitterati and hippies and the boutique I worked in sold beautiful Moroccan and Indian clothes, shoes and jewellery. It was all very glamorous and cosmopolitan.

It was a glorious couple of months, long crazy hazy days on pure white sandy beaches, meeting and mixing with all sorts of famous and exotic people, Italian playboys and royalty from all over Europe. I was dressing in Moroccan robes, with hair down to my waist, and dancing the nights away when I was not working in the club.

I remember one day on the beach meeting this exotic-looking man called Alejandro, a hippy, probably in his mid-thirties with long hair and beard strongly scented with patchouli oil, covered in beads and bangles and fringed leather Indian gear, his hands and ears encrusted with Indian Navajo jewellery. He had two beautiful Afghan hounds called Rubi and Rossa and lived in this bizarre underground cave in the hills, elegantly kitted out with afghan rugs and water mattresses and hammocks. The air was filled with incense; there were crystals everywhere and, of course, very loud rock music. This is where I was offered my first taste of a 'naughty cigarette'. I think I passed out.

Throughout the rest of the holiday I had many adventures, getting into scrapes, swimming for octopus at night, riding in exquisite boy-toy racing boats, waterskiing, moonlight bathing and dancing round campfires on the beach, doing hippy photo shoots for glamorous island magazines and always hanging out with beautiful, exotic people. We were young and drunk or stoned on life. I vowed as that holiday was coming to an end that if I managed to get into drama school I would be coming back the next summer. I did go back, but with dramatically dire results.

It was around the middle of August 1969, a swelteringly hot evening back on the Emerald Coast. I was working through the summer again at Pedro's. It was my night off.

My boyfriend, still Gianni – the same one from the previous year – was on duty in the bar and I was relaxing in the little shack we shared in the hills, away from the main resort, with several others who worked there. I must admit my memory's a little hazy. It was the summer I was really introduced to marijuana. I was alone; the others were working in the club on this particular night. It was stiflingly hot and I was lying naked on a mattress, with an electric fan slowly moving the humid air, listening to Iron Butterfly playing 'In-A-Gadda-Da-Vida' on an ancient turntable and gently under the influence.

Suddenly the door crashed down and there were three gentlemen with levelled guns screaming at me to get up off the bed and stand against the wall. In my halting Italian I asked whether I could get dressed. With their guns they indicated, 'No, get up against the wall!' Amazing how quickly one sobers up in such a situation. By now I was very scared.

They started to ask me where my boyfriend and the others were. I told them they were back at the nightclub, working. Unbeknownst to me they already knew this. The club had been raided and everyone was under house arrest, including my boyfriend. It was no secret that Princess Margaret and Princess Maria Pia di Savoia amongst other world-renowned luminaries were frequent visitors to the nightclub. But obviously anyone of importance or fame was warned to stay away on that fateful night.

They proceeded to tear the little place apart. I honestly had no idea what they were looking for, or indeed who they were. They weren't in uniform, and since it was Sardinia I thought they might well be bandits. But they were police, a self-formed drug squad, tasked with ridding the island of Pedro's.

After ripping mattresses apart and emptying suitcases and destroying what little furniture there was, they ordered me to get dressed. By this time it was about 3.00 a.m. They pushed me into the back of the police car and drove me to the nightclub, where I was reunited with my boyfriend and saw several other friends who had all been detained, including, of course, Pedro and his wife Carol.

For two days we were kept under house arrest. People were body-searched, not allowed to sleep, eat or drink, and kept in the dark as to what was going on. It was only later that I found they had discovered a kilo of marijuana on the premises.

Anyway, after a couple of days eleven of us were arrested, amongst them Pedro, Carol and Kathy, who worked for them, a beautiful lady from the Ivory Coast called Wani, and Mia Martini, who later became a major pop star and twice represented Italy in the Eurovision Song Contest.

Gianni and I were released after a couple of days but they confiscated my passport. Neither of us had any drugs on us. At the time it seemed like a ludicrous adventure. I did not even begin to imagine how serious this was going to turn out to be. I was a British citizen with a British passport, certainly not guilty of anything and with nothing to hide. I felt safe.

I sent a few jokey postcards to friends in the vein of 'you'll never guess what has happened to me' and, just in case, I got in touch with the British consulate in Sassari, one of the island's main towns.

We were given a safe and glamorous place to stay by a very famous Italian playboy of the time called Prince Pignatelli. For three or four days Gianni and I felt as if we were in a bad B-movie. Wherever we went we were shadowed by cops in plain clothes, ducking behind newspapers, hiding round corners and so on. It seemed they were convinced we were going to lead them to some covert international drug ring.

With my passport confiscated I could not leave the island, though I did get in touch with a friend of my father's who had a beautiful villa just down the coast, and he said he could get me to Corsica, which is under French jurisdiction. But, convinced that I had nothing to fear, and wanting to stay with Gianni, I ignored his advice. Very, very stupid.

Several days later, as I arrived in Porto Cervo having arranged to meet the British Consul, I was arrested and taken to the police station. They said that Mia Martini, who had been found with a small amount of marijuana on her person, had told the police I had given it to her. That was totally untrue. But, as I was about to find out, in Italy you were guilty until proven innocent – which, as there was no due process or plausible legal procedure, was nigh-on impossible.

My boyfriend was arrested at the same time. We were in the

same station but in different holding cells. I could hear him shouting to me to be careful what I said. I was truly terrified by this time. This was no longer a silly adventure.

I remember them threatening me with ridiculous things like never seeing my parents again and even being tortured if I didn't tell the truth. And I wasn't even allowed to see the British Consul, who was in the same station at the same time expressly to meet me.

After several hours Gianni and I were loaded into the back of a police car, handcuffed and driven for miles into the interior to a place called Tempio, a circular stone fortress in the middle of nowhere, the country's bandit jail.

We arrived at this imposing and terrifying edifice with gate after gate in its circular stone walls, and we were of course separated. By this time I was hysterical. I was hauled off by a middle-aged female janitor/guardian and put into a cell, where I was kept in solitary confinement for the next two weeks or so.

I could hear the other ladies who had been arrested. They were across the landing and they shouted to me to be brave as I was led to my lonely lock-up, with two windows, one facing inwards and one outwards, both barred. No toilet, just a bucket, and no running water. Just a metal bed that hinged down from the wall.

Though terrified and very alone, I was still naively convinced this could only last a day or so, because I had a British passport. Surely they couldn't hold me without any reason. The British Consul would come and rescue me. How wrong I was. I was there for almost five months.

Those first two weeks were the most frightening. I had no one to talk to. I had no way of telling anyone what had happened. I knew my parents would be beside themselves with worry, my Italian was sketchy and Maria, the guardian who was supposed to help, though sweet and understanding, knew nothing and was meagre comfort. I wasn't allowed contact with the other ladies and, worst of all, there was nothing to do. Many years later in the *Celebrity Big Brother* house I was reminded of those times.

Nothing to read, nothing to occupy my mind apart from the New Testament in Italian and the three-times-daily distraction of food – mornings, warm milk and bread; lunchtimes, pasta or minestrone; evenings, ditto. I had daily meetings with lawyers assigned to us by the Sardinian authorities, who again looked like people from central casting. One of them had an arm missing and always wore a trench coat. He carried a beaten-up typewriter under his good arm.

Day after day they questioned me and said that if I told them what they wanted to hear, things would go easier for me. But I could not give them any information because I knew nothing at all. Of course I admitted to smoking marijuana from time to time when it was offered to me but I had certainly never dealt in the stuff, nor did I know anyone who did. They were convinced that we were all part of a bigger drug-ring picture. Whether there was any truth in that I never found out.

Finally I was allowed to write a letter to my family, but only in Italian as all prison mail was minutely censored. The other terrifying thought that preyed on my mind was that I was due to start drama school in September. Would I lose my place if they found out? What was my family going to say to them so they would still take me if and when I came back to England? As it turned out, possibly thanks to the efforts of my journalist stepfather Nicky and his role at the *Sunday Times*, it didn't get into the press and the drama school never found out; nor did anyone else unless I chose to tell them.

I was about to celebrate my birthday, drama school was starting and there was absolutely no hint as to how long this nightmare could continue. I had heard rumours that if charged I could face eight years in a Sardinian jail. But charged with what?

Slowly I started to receive responses from my wonderful parents and my sister Gaba and a few good friends. When we were finally allowed to receive Italian newspapers they had huge holes in them. Did the stuff they cut out relate to us? My family were amazingly supportive and kind. They started to pull all sorts of strings to try to get mainland lawyers who would drive the whole process along with the help of the Consul and my father's friend on the island. But the Sardinians seemed determined to keep the whole case in their own hands.

I am sad to say all this cost my parents and particularly my darling father a lot of money and, what's much worse, a lot of heartache. They both came to visit me at separate times. I remember it so well. Peering out of the tiny bit of outside window and by way of farewell shouting to my father from high up in the stone tower, and then to my mother and her brother, that I promised once I was out of this hell I would do all in my power to make them proud of me again. Please, please rescue me, I screamed in tears.

Around this time, I wrote to my parents:

From my little cell I can see a tiny patch of blue. It is now five weeks that I have been in here without the sight of a tree or a bird, without feeling the warmth of the sun on my skin, without seeing people walking in the street, without hearing conversation and seeing smiles, all the things we take for granted in a free life. I don't think anyone can understand the beauty of freedom unless they have had it taken away from them for any length of time.

This was of course a ridiculous thing to write to my mother, who knew from her own life far better than me what it was to lose your freedom.

After approximately three weeks the Italian singer Mia Martini was brought in to share my cell with me. In a way it was nice to have company, but I also knew she was the reason I had been arrested in the first place (or so the police said). However, in a situation like that what could one do? At least I had someone to talk to and share fears and sometimes laugh with, and of course my Italian was getting better by the minute. We used to sing and make up appropriate lyrics to well-known pop songs, screaming the words out at the tops of our voices. Through the tiny gap between the bars and the wire-reinforced window which overlooked the areas where the men were led out daily for exercise we would shout to our men friends. Every day we believed that somehow this nightmare was going to end.

After another couple of weeks, all the women were finally put together in one cell, five of us. Carol, who was fiftyish and a wonderful hippy with a mass of blonde Afro hair; Kathy, also English and very hippy, who had tiny twins being looked after by someone not in prison; Wani, the glamorous African wife of a witch doctor on the Ivory Coast, and something of a voodoo queen herself; Mia, the Italian singer. And me. A motley crew.

Eventually we were allowed to have things to do and that made a huge difference. Parents and friends sent us vitamins and shampoo, books and papers to read, knitting wool and embroidery threads, paper and pens to write with, and life settled into a bizarre sort of routine. I remember I made a beautiful little hippy doll for my youngest sister, and cross-stitched two cushion covers for my mother.

We all had these ridiculous prison uniforms to wear, some too big, some too small. The washing facilities were abysmal, the toilet amenities unmentionable, but we still got up to mischief and once even went on strike and refused to wear our uniforms and wandered around for several days in the nude even though no one could see us. We had nowhere to go for fresh air, unlike the men, who had sort of animal pens where they were put out daily. We had one tiny space, part of the warden's flat right up at the top of the tower where we were occasionally allowed up in couples just to get some fresh air. And once we were taken down to the prison chapel for Mass. I don't think I have ever prayed as diligently as I did then.

In such circumstances one does start to look to higher powers. Wani made a Ouija board and we had some quite frightening sessions. She made a doll out of the bread ration, gave it hair stolen from Mia Martini's hairbrush, and put a pin in its throat, and Mia lost her voice for two weeks.

I remember we figured out a way of writing little messages on bits of thin toilet paper. Having emptied the tobacco out of a cigarette we would roll these messages and sort of pea-shoot them through the tiny space in between the bars of the window and the wired window panes to the men in their exercise pens below. Sometimes they figured out ways of sending us messages back stuck in cellophane on the bottom of the huge metal pasta holders that were sent up to us from the kitchens. We had cockroaches and scorpions as occasional cell visitors. And, of course, constant daily interrogation by police and lawyers.

At the beginning of November, when it still looked as if there would be a trial before Christmas, I suddenly developed these strange sores on my arms. The prison doctor said it was due to lack of vitamins and fresh air so it was ordained that I should travel to the main prison in Sassari to be inspected by a proper doctor.

On a public train in my hideous prison dress I was handcuffed by each hand to two police officers. When I needed to visit the bathroom only one handcuff was released, while the other officer remained attached and the door was left open.

In the main prison I was marched past a series of men's open cells to be examined, totally nude, on a doctor's couch surrounded by men with levelled guns. I know it all sounds like make-believe, but it's all true. For the few days I was there I shared a cell with a murderess.

Then there was a brief and totally ludicrous period when, as the result of a misunderstanding, I was accused of being a spy. British police or Interpol were asked whether they knew of my name, which at the time was still Róza Maria Lubienska. They replied that I was not in their records – i.e. criminal records – but the Italians took that to mean I was unknown as a British citizen and therefore my passport was a forgery. This could have added sixteen years on to whatever sentence I might be receiving. As you can imagine, this put me into a total panic.

From the paperwork that passed between my parents, the British Consul and the numerous lawyers, and which I saw later, it all looked as if there was going to be a big trial towards the end of December and the best my parents were given to hope for was a lenient sentence of three or four months. My poor father had to shell out for better lawyers than the ones who were assigned to me by the prison but, as it turned out, we never went to trial. There was an amnesty. Everyone was released on Christmas Eve apart from two of us. Those two had to spend another year in prison.

We were told with only a day or two's warning that we were being released. I was escorted to Rome airport by the police and put on a flight to Munich to see my father. Oh, the joy of that reunion! From there I flew to England to my mother and the rest of the family. It was an unbelievable feeling to be free again and I will always be grateful for their enormous love and understanding throughout this horrendous and terrifying time, not least to my dear sister Gaba who missed out on her twenty-first birthday party because of her elder sister's incarceration.

I was released *con formula piena*, which effectively meant as if I had never been arrested. Sadly, I was also to be *persona non grata* in Italy for ten years. But I had learnt to speak pretty good Italian.

CHAPTER 4

SALVADOR DALÍ'S BEDROOM

When the new term began at the Webber Douglas drama academy I was still banged up in my Sardinian jail and I was terrified that I would lose my place there, along with my bursary and the dream I had nurtured since I was a little girl. But I didn't, thank goodness.

I was welcomed in and, while I was never hugely popular with Raph Jago, who was the principal, I had wonderful support from the very old-school, rather plummy, terribly English vocal coach Sheila Moriarty, who really liked my voice. She thought it was unusual, something to hold on to that would take me out of the general run of other students. In those days, certainly at RADA, you were taught to adjust not only your accent but also your timbre. Even before I became a heavy smoker my voice was dark and low, it's always been like that.

Then there was the question of my name. In those days I was still officially Róza Maria Lubienska, but it was time for a change. It was just too long and complicated. I needed something pronounceable and easily remembered but I did want to retain a slight foreignness. Everyone at drama school already knew me as Rula. I became Rula Lenska.

We had various slightly strange movement classes – one was called Body Control – we had tap, we had fencing (I've only had to fence once in my life, playing Robinson Crusoe on stage). We had movement in costume. We had make-up classes. There were mask classes, which were fascinating. It was a great time.

At the start of drama school I was still living at home but soon, like most other people, I was sharing a flat with a bunch of other girls – or girls and boys – but the cast and location were constantly changing. Sometimes it was mansion blocks with eight, nine or ten people all living in a cramped space – three people in one bedroom. We were like all students everywhere and because I had come from a rather strict upbringing I really let my hair down. I wasn't a great drinker in those days, but I did smoke – and occasionally marijuana, as almost everybody did.

Steven Berkoff was brought in to teach improvisation. He was an extraordinary-looking man, very striking. He was demanding, extreme and quite famous both as writer and performer. His classes were very exciting and also quite scary because he used to push the boundaries in lots of directions. Of course, in those days, like in school or anywhere else, any sort of liaison or relationship between pupil and teacher was strictly forbidden.

Mr Berkoff had a brief liaison with my great friend Krysia who now lives in Poland. I had known her since Polish Brownies and she's godmother to my daughter. One evening she asked me whether I would join them, make up a foursome and surprise him. I said, 'It's going to be no surprise. He's been teaching me for a year.' She said, 'No, no, no. Let's play a good trick on him. Let's disguise you completely.' So I put on a wig and fake eyelashes and fake nails and tinted glasses and dressed in a way I would never normally dress – and I introduced myself to him that evening as 'Rózamaria Laura Leopoldyna Monika Lubienska – but you can call me Kiki'.

So he kissed my hand and we had a great evening together and he never recognised me.

I spoke with a heavy Eastern European accent and never took off my glasses. It was a totally successful performance. Years later, when I met him, I reminded him of this incident. It's something we giggle about every time I see him now.

I never really had a Polish accent – I lost it when I was young and started going to English school – but I was quite good at putting on foreign accents and Sheila Moriarty always said that would be useful, a sort of niche – there would not be that much competition. British regional accents I was never very good at: they didn't sit right with my voice and I always felt uncomfortable about them.

I still believed then that getting a diploma from a drama school would make some sort of difference to getting on in the business – but I don't think anybody has ever asked me about a diploma. How useful was my time there? Certainly what I learnt vocally made a difference. Discipline was taught: how to move, sit and stand in period costume. We did a little bit of television work as well and we learnt the difference between that and playing a character on stage, where everything has to be slightly larger than life because you have to reach the last row in the stalls and the last row in the gods; in television and film, you allow the camera to do the work.

Twice a year there were performances in the little Chanticleer Theatre. Everybody was given the opportunity to play a lead role. Charlotte Cornwell, Antony Sher, Susan Penhaligon and Susan Littler were in my generation. We were all like-minded people wanting to make a career in the theatre, cinema and television. We were finding our feet. I soon found myself a group of friends who remained close right through drama school and some of them for many years afterwards.

For me it was Georgie – Georgina Barker as she was then, later Georgina Melville – Brian Deacon, her then boyfriend who later became my husband, and Donald MacIver. I had a crush on Donald, a very beautiful-looking Scottish actor slightly older than me. We were both in *A Tale of Two Cities* at the open-air theatre in Perranporth in Cornwall. He played Darnay and I played Madame Defarge.

These college productions in the Chanticleer Theatre were important because we were allowed to invite not only friends and family but also potential agents. In those days, because Equity was a closed shop, it was very difficult to get membership if you hadn't done a certain amount of work, and it was difficult to get that certain amount of work if you weren't an Equity member, though thanks to Jack Warner and *Dixon of Dock Green* I did have a provisional Equity card.

Because we were on a three-year course, whatever contacts we managed to make, or whatever sniffs of interest one might get from agents, wouldn't actually bear fruit until the final year. Then they could be very important.

One of my final performances was as Desdemona in *Othello* and they didn't choose a black actor to play Othello, though there was one in our year. So my Othello had to black up for the performance. He was extremely nervous and sweated profusely. I was lying on the bed for the famous throttling scene and he dripped black make-up all over my snow-white nightdress. I looked a total sight by the end of it. The stage had quite a strong rake on it and the bed was on castors, and the block that was supposed to stop the castors didn't work. As he jumped on to the bed, it went crashing against the proscenium arch and actually knocked me out.

The other play we did as a final was about the Cuban revolution, all of us dressed in army fatigues with shirts split down to the waist. My friend Donald was playing Che Guevara.

I was lucky. I got an agent, and a highly respected one too: Elspeth Cochrane, who died only a couple of years ago, well into her nineties. Her partner was a gentleman called Vernon Conway. They asked whether they could take me on immediately after leaving drama school, and very soon I had become Vernon Conway's protégée. He too became a very close friend and I was with him for about twenty-three years.

I got my first job straight after leaving drama school. It was a Francis Durbridge thriller at the Windsor Theatre and it transferred from there to the Fortune Theatre in the West End, running for just over a year. It starred Gerald Harper, who was very suave. He was famous because he was Hadleigh, an Aston Martin-driving squire and hero of a long-running television series. He had an enormous following of middle-aged women. Some of them came to see him in the play again and again. It was called *Suddenly At Home* and I was a two-timing au pair girl with a slightly foreign accent. I shared a dressing room with Penelope Keith, who wasn't very well known yet. She was killed off at the end of the first act. We got on terribly well. She's very funny and she taught me to play bridge.

At that age you're aching to do bits and bobs and travel and discover and broaden your horizons and here I was, stuck doing the same show eight times a week – but I also realised how lucky I was. To get a regular job so soon was pretty unusual and to be in a long run in the West End wasn't to be sneezed at. And I learnt a lot.

While I was at the Fortune I was looking after an enormous Pyrenean mountain dog for a friend of mine: huge, and with a dressing room barely six feet by seven. The dog would have to come into the theatre with me as I had nowhere else to leave him, but he took up half the dressing room and he'd sort of squeeze into my bit of the room. But he was as good as gold, never barked – apart from the first time he heard my voice on stage over the Tannoy. He started howling and apparently it could be heard in the auditorium.

Shortly after that I was at a party with Krysia and there was this very flamboyant-looking, tall, blond, very attractive gentleman called Pavlik Stooshnoff and he told me he was of Russian parentage, quite high aristocracy, but that his family had moved to Canada. He ran a surrealist art gallery in Brook Street and he was very beautiful, at least ten years older than me, extraordinary-looking, wonderfully dressed, always perfectly coiffed and smelling of aftershave. Very sexy. It was love at first sight, a *coup de foudre*. He was at the party with another girl, although I don't think she was a very serious girlfriend, and from that night for the next three years we were inseparable.

He lived in a little flat in the Fulham Road opposite the ABC cinema and he had two little shih-tzu dogs called Proust and Dalí. The gallery was quite successful, mostly dealing in Salvador Dalí and Magritte and Giorgio de Chirico. Pavlik was the frontman. It was actually owned by a Greek, but

Pavlik did all the meeting and greeting and soirées. And he also dealt personally in Surrealist art, so he used to travel abroad; one of his main personal buyers was Imelda Marcos, so he would go off to the Philippines and come back with wonderful presents. He was a very flamboyant, extremely generous man. My family adored him and he had a lot of friends in showbiz. Cat Stevens used to come round to the flat in the evenings to play guitar and jam.

Hanging on our walls we'd have Francis Bacons worth oodles, and Magrittes. We had a huge waterbed but, strangely enough, no proper kitchen. We used to do a lot of entertaining, so everything was catered. When Pavlik sold one of these paintings for thousands and thousands and thousands of pounds, we would live like a king and queen for two or three weeks; out at Tramp every night and the best champagne and caviar. Pavlik was a man who liked his alcohol and he used to get absolutely plastered, though not in an aggressive way – it would start off being comical, then he would just collapse somewhere.

He invited me to go with him to Spain to visit Salvador Dalí in Cadaqués. We were to have tea with him and Gala, his wife. I was terribly excited at the prospect of meeting such a legendary figure and such a very peculiar man. We rang his doorbell on a boiling-hot afternoon and a maid opened the door, dressed from head to foot in white, including the shoes, but with black stockings and black sunglasses. The first thing you saw when you went in was this very lifelike hand coming out of the wall holding a candelabra. At the foot of the stairs was an enormous stuffed bear which looked terribly real.

We were shown into an office full of curiosities and Gala came through dressed in a ballet tutu. She was in her early eighties. She was wearing ballet shoes and her hair scraped up in a bun.

There was a bit of small talk and we had a cup of tea and then the great man himself was shown in. He looked exactly as he did in every picture that you ever saw of him, with his amazing waxed moustache and extraordinary cane, beautifully dressed and with those bizarre eyebrows which shot straight up into his forehead. We went outside for drinks. The famous lips sofa was by the swimming pool and the conversation was fairly stilted, but at one point he said to me, 'I want to show you my bedroom.'

I suppose it was a mildly outrageous proposal but outrage was his art form and the invitation was very elegantly put. I was a little nervous. Everyone knew about his hobbies. We climbed a circular staircase that came up into the middle of an enormous room, with a giant four-poster bed swathed in silks and velvets. Pavlik was with me. Our host suggested a project involving a threesome, the bed and photographs but, greatly to my relief, it remained in the realm of his imagination.

In the second year I was with him, as a birthday present Pavlik bought me a London black taxicab, except mine was actually white and instead of *Taxi* on the front it had *Rula* written on it. I was touring with three shows and the first place we were working in was Westcliff-on-Sea, and of course when everybody found out I had this taxi I was forever ferrying them backwards and forwards, a very lonely business because I was isolated in the front and couldn't join in or hear anything that was going on at the back. Frequently, as I drove through London, people would see this glossy white cab and just jump in the back and say, 'Can you take me to…', and I'd have to say, 'I'm not a real taxicab.' That was great fun.

It turned out Pavlik had been married before, though he kept me in the dark about it for quite a while. He also had an unpredictable character, being eccentric and incredibly jealous. He used to go through my address book and, on one occasion I remember, I had Topo Gigio written down. It was an Italian restaurant, but he was convinced it was an Italian lover. He worked himself up into a fury, thumped me with the telephone and stormed off.

I left and went home to my mother's house and that was the end of it. Next day, a hundred red roses arrived. He was very upset and begged for forgiveness and promised that everything was going to change, everything was going to get better. I felt slightly mixed emotions. We had a great time together but I was angry and upset and I knew our relationship wasn't going to go anywhere.

He now lives in Canada and I am still in touch with him. We are good friends and he is convinced that we are two old twin souls who will get back together again.

Rock Follies: *Julie Covington, Charlotte Cornwell and me.*

CHAPTER 5

MY ROCK FOLLIES

It was 1975. I was twenty-eight years old and I had been a jobbing actress since leaving drama school, with fairly good, steady work: guest appearances in television specials and a lot of touring. Then, suddenly, my agent rang me up: 'Thames Television are casting for a series.'

The working title was *Rock Follies* and it was about a girl rock group. My immediate fear was that, although I love singing and come from a family where singing and music were always a large part of life, I did not consider myself a good solo singer. My big forte is harmonising, which all Eastern Europeans know how to do.

My agent said the programme had really good acting scripts by Howard Schuman. I had done a television play written by him up in Granada, where I was some sort of sci-fi Miss Universe, so I had met him. There were songs being specially written by Andy Mackay from Roxy Music, who also happened to be one of my idols at the time.

The initial meetings were always in front of Andrew Brown and Verity Lambert (the two main producers), Andy Mackay and his wife Jane, and David Toguri (our main choreographer), Howard Schuman and several directors from Thames.

I remember the first audition. I don't remember if Charlotte Cornwell was there but Julie Covington was there from the beginning. There were different permutations of girls called in to see how they acted with each other and how the different personalities and looks matched the three characters. The singing auditions were really the scariest, as Julie had the most wonderful voice – she was already a solo artist in her own right. I knew Charlotte Cornwell quite well because we had been at drama school together but I thought that because we were two redheads there was no way we were both going to get cast. Surely they would want a brunette or a blonde.

I was up for the part of Nancy Cunard de Longchamps, known as Q – from a very well-heeled background, with a bossy mother and a bit of money. The Anna character (Charlotte's) was a university student, very much a *cause* person, married to a university professor. She also had a very bossy mother. Devonia was a sort of commune rock chick – that was Julie, with the spiky hair.

Each time we met to audition we would do a bit of reading, a bit of singing and a bit of dancing. And, obviously, after the third or fourth time, you think: 'I've got to be in with a chance.'

We knew that this was going to be a big series, we knew it was important and that there was going to be a lot of money spent on it but none of us had any idea quite what a thing it would become.

The auditions always took place in the Serbian Community Centre just off Ladbroke Grove, an enormous hall with a piano. Because we already knew each other Charlotte and I became very close. But I was impressed by Julie because she was very funky, very streetwise and very confident and she had this extraordinary, beautiful voice. Her version of 'Don't Cry For Me Argentina' still makes me cry.

Eventually – I think it was after audition number five – they announced to us that we had finally got these parts. I was terrifically excited. I just had to rush out and tell as many people as possible. I jumped into the nearest phone box and rang my agent, and I rang my mother, and I rang my sister and I rang my then boyfriend Brian, who was to become my first husband. Just shrieking, 'I got it, I got it, I got it, I got it, I got it.' Then we all went off to Julie's, a trendy restaurant in Notting Hill, to celebrate – Howard, Andy, the producers and us three girls.

When proper rehearsals started they were morning till night. We did nothing but eat, think, learn lines, practise songs and learn the dance routines. It was all-consuming. And the wonderful thing was that right from the very beginning we all had an input. Howard Schuman, the writer, was there all the time and if we felt something wasn't quite how our character would say it he would always take that into account. In the first series it was us – the Little Ladies – against the world as we struggled to make a name for ourselves; in the second series it was war within the Little Ladies, and as time went on some of the same tensions and jealousies developed between us three actresses, or from us two towards Julie. That was tricky, but useful for the show.

Basically, in the very first episode, the three girls are rehearsing for a schmaltzy musical called *Broadway Annie* and the show goes on the road. Anna, the university student (Charlotte Cornwell), gets the lead role and Julie and myself are the soubrettes – and it's a dreadful show and a total flop. But as we are sitting in a pub with Hyper Huggins (played by Emlyn Price), who was supposed to be managing us and writing the music, he suddenly says: 'You know, I think you three girls have got something together, I think you could maybe make a go at trying to become a rock group.'

In those days, in real life, a big British female rock group wasn't something that had happened. In a way, we were the Spice Girls of that generation. So the first half of the first series was about the Little Ladies trying to find their way and working out what sort of music they were going to sing and what they were going to look like. They started off wearing tight jeans and boots, and leather belts and leather jackets – quite Suzi Quatro. And of course it was immediately apparent in rehearsals, and in the storyline, that Dee (the Julie Covington character), was always going to be the lead singer.

We all got bits and pieces but Charlotte and I did most of the backing vocals. I got on incredibly well with Andy, so I had as much harmony written in as possible.

One of the things that developed in the second series was my love affair with Harry Moon (played by Derek Thompson, who has been in *Casualty* for years and years). And a strange sort of love affair it was, because though Q (my character) didn't know it, Harry Moon was gay.

As it happens this mirrored, extraordinarily, my drama school relationship with Don MacIver, one of my little group of nearest and dearest. I was madly in love with him and he was in love with me. We would lie in bed holding hands and I used to think, 'What's wrong with me, why doesn't he fancy me?' and he was thinking, 'Why don't I fancy her?' He didn't know he was gay and I didn't know he was gay; we are very good friends to this day.

Q was a perfect part for me. She had a head that was somewhere back in the thirties. She dressed in extraordinary vintage clothes and talked old-fashioned language: 'I want to be a Topper girl.' She was also in many ways what I think I used to be in those days – quite flamboyant, not very hip and certainly not savvy about rock music. She was appearing in soft-core porn movies to make money for the group so they could carry on and she tried to force the other girls to be in them too. I certainly wasn't doing that in real life.

I remember feeling 'this is what I've come into the business for'. It was a terrific buzz to know that for the first time, after five or six years, I was in a hit series. Every time we went into the studio we saw how much effort and money was being expended on the extraordinary costumes and make-up and the fantasy sequences. They wanted it to be a flagship show for Thames Television. Over the months there was mounting excitement and a realisation that we really did have something very special.

I vividly remember the thrill of coming into these enormous sets at Thames. In every single episode there were big fantasy sequences. One of the first was called 'Stairway': they had built these three enormous staircases going right up into the rafters of the studio, with no sides and no rails, huge, long white staircases disappearing into nothing.

We were in full evening dress with very high stiletto heels and I will never forget going up sideways, obviously not looking where I was going (or at least not supposed to be looking) and being absolutely terrified, trying to keep my balance in my high heels, trying not to tread on the dress, trying to remember the lines, trying to look glamorous. Julie always seemed to be able to do this without any problem. She was awesome, she really was.

Everybody was abuzz about this series – from the make-up people to the wardrobe people, to the crew. And we had incredible costumes that were designed for us in Abba-type stretch Lycra, and fantastic wigs. And we did all our own singing. A lot of people think session singers had been brought in to do the music but it was us, all of it was us.

There were always slight niggles between us three girls, right from the very beginning. Julie was not the easiest person to get close to. She knew how good she was and she knew how good her voice was and I think there were times when she slightly resented the fact that she was part of a threesome. We didn't see an enormous amount of each other socially; every single day was either rehearsing or in the studio, for two years as it turned out. I was openly in awe of Julie. Charlotte was slightly more prickly about it, and she certainly had a better voice than I had but it was a sort of operatic light musical voice rather than a rock voice.

We had our own band, all extremely good session musicians who played live with us in most of the episodes. When we recorded later for the albums, there would be Andy Mackay playing the sax and various other people coming in to do fuller musical versions, but it was always us singing. We weren't always singing live on the floor when we were recording the episodes, sometimes we were miming to backing tracks, but obviously it was our voices.

I was paid something like £700 an episode, which was not a lot of money, but we didn't have anything to gauge it against. I was living with Brian, my husband-to-be, just off the Fulham Road in a tiny little flat full of Indian and Afghan fabrics and candles and incense – totally hippy, which I've always been and still am to a certain extent. His own career was going well but he was immensely helpful. Being able to come home to somebody to help you learn the lines and to talk to about things was marvellous. He was a great, good, supportive person.

My parents were still coming to terms with me being an actress. They had seen me in the theatre in some pretty good stuff, Shakespeare included, but a television series, particularly about a rock group, was certainly not my father's idea of something to be terribly proud of.

In the evenings we would rehearse for the album and put down tracks. Julie was a veteran, obviously, but this was my first proper experience of being in a grown-up, bona fide recording studio. That was thrilling, but nerve-racking too and you were exhausted after rehearsing all day with the acting and the dancing, and then going into the studio to sing. If you're not a singer and if you don't have great confidence and you hear

Julie's flawless voice through the headphones, there are lots of reasons to feel very uncertain about yourself.

I remember there was a bit of drinking. I didn't drink in those days at all. And the odd bit of pharmaceutical help, like ProPlus: caffeine certainly picks you up when you're on your knees. There were moments when we felt as if we were proper rock stars, or part of a proper rock group – not just the characters. And of course Andy Mackay was with us and Roxy Music were hugely popular then. Andy had hair down to his waist and his wife Jane, who became a close friend of mine, had hair down to her waist as well – half of it was dyed white and it had different coloured tips on the end of it. Very glamorous and flamboyant.

It was without doubt the most exciting time in any job I've ever done on a long-term basis. And when the last of the first series was filmed and in the can we went all over the country with Andy to promote *Rock Follies*, doing bits of singing but mostly interviews for magazines and newspapers.

And then the first episode came out. I can't remember where I watched it. I think it might have been at home with a bunch of friends and family and I remember thinking, 'Wow. This is really good.' The music was fantastic. There were great songs, terrific lyrics and we sounded like a real rock group.

The following morning I had to go to Sainsbury's and I was only twenty yards out of my house, coming on to the main

Fulham Road, when people were stopping me and saying, 'Oh, weren't you in the *Rock Follies* last night? It's amazing, fantastic. May I have your autograph? May I take a photograph?'

And from that first day, from that first episode being broadcast, life changed. Suddenly, one felt obliged to appear in public with the full hair and make-up and no longer go out bleary-eyed in grubby jeans with mascara smeared down one's face.

Very soon after the first episode was aired we were back to do the second series. Obviously, knowing we had a hit on our hands bucked us all up. But as soon as we saw how the storyline was moving, and that the Little Ladies were taken over by a pushy female agent, it was obvious that Julie was being pushed very much into the foreground, and Charlotte and I were being relegated to harmony queens.

And it wasn't just the singing. It was true of the episodes as a whole. Julie had more and more to do. For example, as part of the storyline one of our characters' voices would be overdubbed by Julie without us knowing – then this actually happened in reality as well.

There was a fair bit of jealousy and the fear that Charlotte and I were going to get pushed out of it altogether. Then they brought in another girl – tiny, petite, dark-haired Sue Jones-Davies – who had a similar kind of rock voice to Julie and that made us even more scared.

We probably weren't as open about our feelings as we should have been. I remember talking to Howard Schuman about it from time to time but I was never very good at confronting Julie and saying to her that as an actress and a character in the story she should be defending us, her partners, not welcoming this new bird in with open arms.

Then, because in the storyline we were taken over by this female agent, they kept changing our image. We were no longer rock chicks. We went from being 1930s divas, which was right up my street, to being Second World War Vera Lynn-type characters and we got pushed from pillar to post, exactly as happens in the rock world, and indeed in the acting world. Charlotte was always slightly more vociferous than me and much more able to fight her corner.

To my mind, the first series, when it was the Little Ladies against the rest of the world, was stronger and the music was better. The second series was more flamboyant. The use of television techniques was really pushed to its limits. We had some amazing guests appearing, amongst them Tim Curry playing a drug-addled, very cruel, famous rock star. And of course it became massive in this country and in Australia. It didn't get shown on network television in America, only on PBS.

We were in a studio somewhere, doing an interview, when Andy Mackay's wife started making signals from behind the plate-glass window, where she was in the listening area, to tell us that our single 'O.K?' was in the top ten and that the first album had just gone platinum in Australia. And then we won a BAFTA.

Discussions began about the third series and it became fairly obvious that Julie was not keen on continuing because she didn't want to carry on being part of a threesome, preferring to concentrate on her solo career and acting. I remember feeling at the time desperately let down. I thought this had a further life, but again, I never had it in me to confront Julie and say 'Don't you think it might be nice to do just one more series?'

We could never understand why *Follies* wasn't very quickly repeated, either on terrestrial television or on one of the satellite channels. It turned out that the premise of the story originally was put forward by three actresses Diane Langton, Gaye Brown and Annabel Leventon, who had a group themselves called Rock Bottom. They had apparently come to Howard with this idea and they had been told that if it did ever get off the ground, they would be cast.

I don't know for certain the reasons why this didn't happen but I do know that Diane Langton was under contract to do *A Little Night Music* in the West End. Maybe they didn't want to cast two and get in a third one, so they cast three completely new girls. The Rock Bottom girls then sued both

Thames Television and Howard personally and won, and I believe that's one of the reasons why this series has never been repeated in this country.

Alberto VO5 hair.

CHAPTER 6

'WHO THE HELL IS RULA LENSKA?'

For a time in America I was the most famous person nobody had ever heard of. The embodiment of glamour, the goddess of hair, *Rula Lenska, international star of stage, screen and TV.*

Immediately after *Rock Follies* I was contracted by an American company, Alberto VO5, emperors of haircare, to do a series of commercials for US television. Actually, some of them were shown here, most of them were filmed here, and I think I filmed four in America. There were about sixteen of them. They were little vignettes and you don't see commercials like that any more. Each one was like a short excerpt from a film, using one of the products – the hairspray, the conditioner or the hot oil treatment. It was me coming down the steps of a plane looking a million dollars, me in a very grand dressing room and so on, tossing my hair, which is, I must admit, of international stature.

I'm not sure whose idea it was, but at the end of each of these little films there would be a caption saying what an enormous star I was. It was a big campaign, many millions of Americans must have seen it, but nobody in America knew me. I had never done anything there. I think I did look glamorous and my hair certainly looked good but the idea of selling me as 'an international star' was a sort of camp joke.

I became a minor cult figure. I even made it on to *The Johnny Carson Show*, though not quite in person. Carson asked his vast audience: 'Who the hell is Rula Lenska?' Suddenly there were clubs springing up in the States and Rula Lenska lookalike days.

Steve Allen, who was a very famous comic with his own hour-long review show, was doing a take-off of me, dressed in a long animal-print kaftan, sitting in front of a mirror with little light bulbs round it, wearing a wig of very long and curly red hair, saying something like, 'I'm always going to use Alberto V05 to make my voice darker.' They decided to fly me over to surprise him on his show. I stepped out from behind this mirror and said: 'Excuse me, you're not Rula Lenska, I am.' And he got such a fright that he backed away from me – for some reason there was a swimming pool on the set – and he fell straight into the pool in full costume and they had to send divers down. He really didn't know. It was a complete surprise. And that has been on any number of *Pardon My Blooper*-style out-take shows of unusual things that have happened on television, both here and in America, ever since.

My trip to America was all very strange. We were picked up by stretch limo from Los Angeles airport and put up at the Beverly Wilshire Hotel and I was actually treated like the world-famous star I was supposed to be.

Doing commercials was not a great part of my vision of being a successful actress, but the money, I thought then, was wonderful. In fact, having talked to a lot of people who were more experienced about commercials money, I should have made ten times as much as I actually did. My dear agent, bless him, had no great knowledge about American fees. But while I was there I met film producers and directors and major film stars, and it really looked as if something was going to happen – *Follies* hadn't been big in America but the people who had watched the public broadcasting channel knew about it.

There was vague talk about television series and I went to meet some agents, and I was being persuaded to stay there for a bit to go up for casting sessions, but by then I was married and had an eight-month-old daughter back at home and I certainly couldn't afford to bring the whole family to the States, so I returned to England.

I really never have been climbing-over-people ambitious, but if that had been the priority in my life I'd have stayed there, and who knows? Maybe a career in America would have developed. But as I was back here nothing was ever likely to happen. As my British agent said: 'Everywhere it's out of sight, out of mind, but even more so in America.' You had to be on the spot, and in those days Equity and green cards were much, much more difficult to get hold of.

But there were a few US things that were bandied about from time to time. In the eighties there was talk of me being in *The Colbys*, the follow-on from *Dynasty*. But I seem to remember they wanted it written into the contract that it would be the production company who would decide when and if one was to have cosmetic enhancement. I was in my thirties, and I was completely shell-shocked by this. If anybody was going to decide about that sort of thing it was going to be me and not somebody else. And – again hearsay – it was between three people. In the end Stephanie Beacham got the part.

I have never understood why good-looking middle-aged women aren't used in commercials trumpeting wrinkle-reducing creams and hair rescue products. Not so long ago, I asked my agent to contact Chicago, where Alberto Vo5 were based, since I've still got good hair and people always remark on it. Wouldn't it be a nice idea to do a follow-up thirty years down the line, based on environmental packaging and clean products, which the Americans are terribly keen on, reliving the commercials that were such a cult then?

So far nobody has bitten. I don't imagine the original people who cast me are around any more, because they weren't young even then. So nothing ever happened and nothing has happened since in America, sadly, although people occasionally ring me up and say they've seen one of the commercials. It's part of another era and people still remember them.

But nowadays in America 'Who the hell is Rula Lenska?' is a question few people would even think of asking.

Welcome fellow Rula-lovers, to the Official
INTERPLANETARY HEADQUARTERS OF THE UNIVERSE
DIVISION OF
THE

Rula Lenska Fan Club

THE RULA LENSKA FAN CLUB CODE OF UNWRITTEN RULES TO LIVE BY

1. A Rula Fan must pause whenever possible to
   admire The Fair One as she appears on television
   in any commercial, reguardless of product.

2. A Rula Fan must be able to quote The Fair
   One whenever asked. Her most important lines
   worth quoting: "I'm showing some friends
   around London!" "I'm Ruuulaa Lenzzka..."

3. A Rula Fan must spread the word of The Fair
   One to all unknowing pleebes who remain in
   a cloud of hair spray not having 14-hour hold.

4. A Rula Fan must carry his/her/it's official
   club card, and present it to all interested
   friends, family, loved-ones, soldiers and cops.

5. A Rula Fan is always a Rula Fan, unless The
   Fair One appears on BOWLING FOR DOLLARS.

*** *** *** ***

©1979 R.L.F.C.

The strange 'rules' of the Rula Lenska fan club.

With my first husband, Brian, and our daughter Lara, 1979.

CHAPTER 7

BRIAN, LARA AND ME

I had met Georgie Barker (later Melville) at boarding school and all through drama school she was my dearest friend. The two of us and Brian Deacon and Donald MacIver were very much a sort of foursome. Don's a very clever man who never made it very far in the acting business, but he's a superb teacher. He remains a dear friend and is godfather to my daughter. He fell in love – here in this country – with a Colombian boy called Jairo Castillo, moved to Colombia soon afterwards and has been there ever since.

Georgie and Brian were an item for quite a long time, until she met her husband-to-be, Rory. After Brian and Georgie split up he and I remained close. I was very fond of him but there was no sign of any romance. He seemed to have a string of exotic girlfriends from all over the world.

Poor Georgie became ill. She was diagnosed with multiple sclerosis. I used to take her regularly for treatment to Gunnersbury in west London. where my half-brother was studying acupuncture with a Dr Liu. But her condition quickly worsened and other problems became evident.

It was an incredibly stressful period for Brian and me, and for everyone else who loved her. We would visit her often and the intensity of it all and the shared distress brought Brian and me closer together. My relationship with Pavlik was coming to an end. I suppose it was a sort of rebound situation at first, but to cut a long story short Brian and I got to know each other much better. We started seeing more of each other. The friendship turned into a romance around 1975.

His parents were both Irish and they lived in Oxford. He had two brothers and a sister. I remember so well the regular visits down to see them. Eileen and Bobby, his mother and father, were absolutely enchanting and warm and welcoming. His older brother Robert had moved to America by then but his younger brother Eric was still very much in evidence and so was his sister Cecilia, who was already married and had a child. I got on very well with them.

Then I got *Midsummer's Night Dream* at the open-air theatre in Regent's Park, playing Titania, and Brian went off to India, I think with the British Council, to do *Rosencrantz and Guildenstern Are Dead* and I realised while he was away how very much I missed him. When he came back we decided we were going to be the love of each other's life and that maybe we should get married.

My mother adored Brian, the whole family did. Not only

Leliwa: the Tarnowski family coat of arms.

My grandmother (Babi), with Lula,
Jaś and Mama.

My mother Bisia (far right) and her siblings.

The grand salon at Dzików, with my mother on her mother's knee.

My parents' wedding in Rome, 1946.

General Anders and my father.
©Press Association

My christening: on Babi's knee, with my father (top right) and mother (standing).

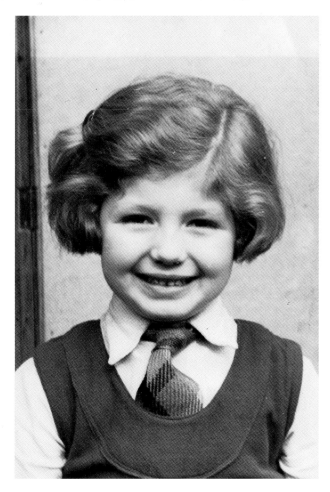

Aged six, at the Jesus and
Mary Convent.

My father, with me and Gaba, 'The Beat Girls', at the annual Polish Immigration Ball.

My friend Veronica Hammond (left) and Mother Mary of the Incarnation (centre) at the Ursuline Convent, Westgate-on-Sea.

With the flamboyant
Pavlik.

With the Amazonian
chief and Wladek.

My father, in
uniform, at my first
wedding in 1977.

With Diesel (as Dennis was called by many at the time).

Mr and Mrs Waterman: our Aboriginal wedding in Queen's Park, Perth, 1987.

Our breathtaking hot-air balloon ride over the Masai Mara.

Pretending to be a Masai.

The Three Sisters: Rula, Anna and Gaba.

My brother Andrew and his gorgeous wife Jacqui.

was he very handsome and talented and a real gentleman, he was just great fun to be with. When she was due to meet Brian's parents for the first time shortly before the marriage, my mother asked Brian to tell her a typically Irish phrase that she could surprise them with. Eileen and Bobby were coming to the house in Teignmouth Road for Sunday lunch and Brian said to my mother, 'Oh this is very Irish and this will really make my parents laugh – "Bejesus, begorrah, me old cock, me old beauty."'

So my mother practised this over and over again and wrote it down phonetically. Although her command of the English language was excellent, she did have a very strong Polish accent. I remember the moment they arrived, the doorbell went and the door opened and Bobby, Brian's dad, who was very small, was greeted by my mother's heavily accented 'Bejesus, begorrah, me old cock, me old beauty,' and his face was a total picture. At first he just couldn't believe it and then he burst into laughter and it was a fantastic icebreaker.

Our wedding was almost immediately after *Follies*, so the press were very much on the case and one of the *Follies* designers made my dress: ivory silk, cut on the bias, very 1940s with a train and an old lace veil. The ceremony was in Brompton Oratory, where a Polish priest, Father Kirszke, a great friend of the family, had christened me. The whole ceremony was in Polish, which was a bit of a mistake (not ideal for Brian's Irish family). One of our friends, called Stevo, had a beautiful old-fashioned white Bentley and he drove us in the full chauffeur's outfit. And I remember we put together a tape of our favourite music for when we were driving away from the church to the reception, and I'm not quite sure why we chose it but 'Hotel California' was our signature tune at the time.

Then we had a wonderful reception behind Shepherd Market in Mayfair – the Grosvenor Rooms. It was very glossy with a lot of Polish speeches and a few English speeches. Then we went off for a very brief weekend of country-house-hotel luxury at Chewton Glen in Hampshire.

My father, as a wedding present, paid for our honeymoon trip to go and visit my closest friend Veronica, who lived in Kenya, to stay with her and her husband Franco and daughters Claudia and Francesca, the latter being one of my many godchildren. They had a huge ranch called Athi River about thirty miles outside Nairobi, plus a place they rented on the coast, plus a house in Nairobi itself.

Brian and I flew out there and we had the most beautiful three weeks staying with them, with a trip on horseback up Mount Kenya, which I don't think you can do any more, with this wild woman called Amber-May.

It was a real adventure. We were camping at night. There were six of us, plus the crew and Amber-May herself, on these specially trained mountain ponies. The pack animals were zebroids, which are a cross between a zebra and a mule. You couldn't ride on them but they looked absolutely fantastic, like a gold and black version of a zebra. For the first two or three days we were trekking on horseback. It was quite scary, quite steep – a lot of shale. At night they would put the tents up and cook the most extraordinary meals and even put hot water bottles in our sleeping bags. In the morning, the glass of water by your bed would be frozen.

The last two days we were on foot. I remember not being able to make the last 500 or 600 metres. I had a splitting headache and my eyes were not focusing properly. It was the first time I had experienced altitude sickness. It had its tricky moments but, all in all, it was an absolutely magical honeymoon.

The first house we bought was in Gladstone Road, Wimbledon. It was a little end-of-terrace place and we were very happy. We made a good married couple, Brian and I. We had a big social life and a wide range of friends and we used to do a lot of entertaining. We had a really wonderful shared group of friends and I was still seeing Andy Mackay and his wife and Charlotte Cornwell from *Rock Follies* days.

My status after *Follies* certainly changed. Within a year I was being asked to do nice guest appearances on the top television programmes, plus really good shows on the road. A year and a half after we got married we were on location in Israel. Brian was playing Jesus in *The Gospel According to St Luke*. One of the producers was Topol. It was a film for schools, very true to the life of Christ, and Brian made a beautiful Jesus. I was playing Herod's wife Herodias. Our daughter was conceived on the Sea of Tiberius in Galilee, the offspring of one of the most unlikely couplings in biblical history.

A lot of people I knew were in their late twenties or early thirties like me and they all seemed to be having babies at the same time. One whose child was born within three weeks of mine was Jane, Andy Mackay's wife. When I found out I was pregnant I was over the moon and so were both families. Throughout my life I have suffered with a dicky back, on and off, constantly seeing chiropractors and osteopaths. And one of the bonuses of getting pregnant was that I felt fantastic and the backache went completely for the whole nine months, something to do with the alteration of weight and balance. I looked and felt really good, never suffered a moment of sickness or anything like that and never got too huge. I was incredibly excited about the idea of us having the baby. We could have found out whether it would be a boy or a girl, but we never thought of doing that.

I was five months pregnant, and honestly you could hardly see anything, when I was offered Noël Coward's *Design for Living* for television. Everything was 1930s and cut on the bias; it all had to be made specially and I was to wear a corset, but you would never have known. I think that's the last proper job I did, because from around six months I did start to show.

My baby was due in August of 1979. I was going to antenatal classes with a lady called Betty Parsons, who was famous
for having given antenatal classes to Princess Diana and to the
Queen. She was somewhere off Bond Street. Lara was born
in Wimbledon in St Teresa's Maternity Hospital, run by nuns,
which doesn't exist any more. You might have thought I would
have had enough of nuns by then. I was absolutely determined
that I wasn't going to have any pain control. I had done all
the antenatal stuff and Brian had been with me towards the
end and knew all about the singing and breathing and I was
completely up for all of that.

Unfortunately Lara was about three weeks late, so finally
I had to be induced. Within about two hours of the induc-
tion process starting I was screaming for everything that they
could give me and I did have an epidural, but it didn't work
and all I got was tingling in my feet. The birth was wonderful and Brian was there, and she was just perfect. In those
days they used to keep you in hospital for four or five days to
give you a rest – now they shove you out as fast as they can.
I remember the last breastfeed at night was something like
nine o'clock and then they would take the babies away into the
night nursery rather than leaving them with you.

Throughout the five days in hospital I didn't see my baby
till morning and I thought, 'This is a doddle, she's being fed at
nine o'clock then sleeping right through the night.' I couldn't
believe it. So I leave hospital, go back home and feed her at

nine o'clock; two hours later, 'waah, waah, waah'. Feed her again; two hours later: 'waah, waah, waah'. Then I found out that during the time she had been put into the nursery, they had fed her not with supplementary milk but water and glucose. She had been used to being given something every time she woke up. So it was a short-lived euphoric time and in fact she suffered from terrible colic. For the first two years of her life she never slept longer than two or three hours at a stretch.

After three months we found the enchanting, magical Denise Wickstead, known to this day as Nanny Nese. She was the archetypical Mary Poppins. She wasn't a fully trained nanny but she had looked after her brothers and sisters and was just one of life's pearls. She was just fantastic.

Lara never had ready-made baby foods. Everything was freshly cooked and Moulinexed for her. Nanny Nese was the sort who with the best possible motives might end up running your life. She wasn't living in, she would come in on an almost daily basis. She couldn't believe that this little child, beaming, happy and so good-natured throughout the day could be such a horror at night. So she started staying over and learnt how true it was soon enough. In the end she spent nearly a year with us.

My first job after the birth was a Fay Weldon short story dramatised for television called *Watching Me, Watching You*. It was filmed in Bath. Lara was nine months old. In fact, she starred in it, and as Brian was in it too it was a real family performance. We hired a sweet little Victorian cottage and of course Nanny Nese came down too. I was trying to wean Lara, though really I desperately didn't want to stop breastfeeding because I loved it and it was so easy. You didn't have all the palaver of bottles and all that. Lara was the most delightful, bubbly child. She didn't see the need to walk or even move much before she was well over a year old. She was wonderful with company, wonderful when she was being left with my mother or with Brian's parents. I hated leaving her for any length of time, but it was gorgeous to go off and have a short romantic dinner knowing that she was either with my mother or one of the sisters was babysitting.

My sister Gaba had got married to an English orthopaedic doctor and was living also in Wimbledon, quite close to me, and she had her first baby, Marc. I would see my parents and siblings and all of Brian's family on a regular basis and we were quite a happy little family unit. We had a sweet house and an adored little black cat called Koshka. She had piercing amber eyes and a friendly nature – until the arrival of Lara, when she suddenly turned into a witch. She used to wait for me at the bottom of the stairs, which had no proper banister, and try to ambush me by clipping me around the legs whenever I came down carrying the baby. If I put the baby down anywhere, the cat would try and sit on her face – obviously jealousy. We kept the cat for a bit longer but then we had to rehouse her because she was really getting dangerous.

After a year, Nanny Nese had become very, very tied to us and her own personal life was beginning to suffer because she wanted to be with us all the time and she, like everybody, was in love with little Lara. We decided it was better for her if we allowed her to go before she became too involved for her own good. It was a very sad time because she really was an extraordinary woman, and to this day remains a friend to me and to Lara.

When Lara was just over a year old we decided to move to a slightly bigger house. Our house in Gladstone Road had two bedrooms, but the second bedroom was really only a box room – a baby's room. We moved to Cannon Hill Lane, which was the Merton side of Wimbledon. The house was considerably larger, with a bigger garden and a big green playing field area right opposite, and a much bigger mortgage. We were both making reasonable money but, as always with actors, it was spasmodic. Brian was wonderful at DIY and I quite liked cooking and being a housewife, at least for short periods of time, but then I used to miss the job and the travelling around, the way that one does, particularly in theatre, getting to know groups of people and working together – everybody working towards putting a play on.

One of the jobs I remember very well came when Lara was just over a year old. It was *Private Schulz*, a brilliant comedy drama for BBC television. All my bits were filmed in Scotland with the delightful Ian Richardson and Michael Elphick (who are both dead now). Nanny Nese and baby Lara came with me on location. In those days, when Lara was still young enough, and whenever it was possible, I would take her touring and filming with me.

Brian and I were happy; we had a really good relationship. I think towards the end of Lara's second year I was working more and Brian was working less. He loved being with Lara and he was terribly good at it – every aspect of it. But already then, I had moments of conscience: shouldn't the work come second to being around as a mother? But I trusted Brian implicitly and of course we had nannies and Lara never suffered from the fact I wasn't there on a regular basis.

Apart from the fact that the physical side of the marriage suffered, as with all new parents, because of the birth of the baby, there wasn't anything wrong. Maybe, looking back on it, I'd become complacent in some way. I can't explain what happened except to say I've always chased adventure and danger.

Though our marriage was ended by me, Brian was very kind and I'm incredibly grateful. He has always been a wonderful father to Lara. He married a woman twenty years his junior and sadly that broke up and, since then, we have become much, much closer. And it's almost like being a family again. He always comes to me for Christmas, for special birthdays and for weekend lunches when Lara and her family are here. We're very, very close friends now. Lovely.

With Dennis at Live Aid, 1985. (© *Brian Aris*)

CHAPTER 8

FOR THE LOVE OF DENNIS

The very first time I saw Dennis Waterman was in summer 1980 at a charity cricket match in Richmond. Lara was a baby in a pushchair and I had to start the match. His roles as Detective Sergeant George Carter, John Thaw's Flying Squad partner in *The Sweeney*, and as Terry McCann, likeable body-guard to dicey dealer Arthur Daley (George Cole) in *Minder*, had made him a rough-tough-jack-the-lad national hero. It wasn't my kind of television so I didn't realise quite how famous he was but he was certainly very warm and friendly and I could immediately see how loved and admired he was by the people playing with him and by the public.

Not long afterwards I was asked to do a guest appearance on *Minder* and there was definitely an attraction. Our on-screen encounter – in an episode called 'The Birdman of Wormwood Scrubs' – was straight to the point. I was playing a crook's rather smart daughter with a deal to offer: 'I think we ought to have a little cocktail, Terry,' I say … 'Why?' … 'A proposition'

… 'Sexual, I hope,' says Terry … 'You never know,' my character replies. It was broadcast in February 1982. The commentary
under the clip on YouTube says 'the sexual chemistry that set
televisions ablaze'.

In real life the relationship started rather more subtly. I
didn't think Dennis was particularly good looking but he did
have enormous charisma and he was a terrible flirt. And every
evening the crew from the show, not so much the cast, would
go out for drinks after filming, but I was not a drinker in those
days and I had the baby to get back to. Then one evening – I
think my husband was away working – I thought, 'Why not?'

So I joined Dennis and a few others, along with his minder
(even Minders have minders). He was a chap called Barrel who
was also his stand-in and his driver. Everyone called Dennis
by his nickname, Diesel (because a lot of diesel-engine trucks
were made by a firm called Dennis). Soon enough he was to
become my Diesel.

We were at a bar near where we were filming. He was
perched on a stool. There was nowhere for me to sit and I
was sort of standing behind him and he shifted himself to
give me room to sit next to him. He embarked on a drinking session. I was having a good time and joining in with the
conversation although it was pretty laddish. Eventually his
driver said he had to go home and I said, 'It's fine, I'll drive
Dennis back,' because I hadn't been drinking.

We were gently flirting with each other but nothing extra-ordinary. We went via my house. We sat in the kitchen, opposite each other, and we just became fixated, staring into each other's eyes. Then he held my hand and said he felt incredibly strongly attracted to me and I said, 'Well, yes, I have to say I feel the same but we're both married with kids.' There was nothing more than that. I drove him home and dropped him off by his house in Richmond. I didn't see him for a few days but I couldn't get him out of my head and I realised I was beginning to get into dangerous territory.

Then we were filming again and he sent me some hand-written bits of poetry and I sent him some back. The people on the set were clearly aware of it. A lady in hairdressing who had been working with him for a long time and adored him, as everybody did, said to me, 'I warn you, I've seen this happen before. Be careful.'

My marriage was going through a slightly tricky period. Our baby was just over a year-and-a-half old and after you have a child the life you have with your partner is never quite the same, certainly not for the first few years. And certainly not from the point of view of sex.

You just lose interest in that for quite a while because the body becomes like a temple to the child. It might also have had to do with the fact that my career was sort of moving strongly and his was moving not quite so strongly. Although he never complained about that, I think that kind of situation is difficult for a man.

The attraction between Dennis and me was definitely growing. So after my work on the episode was finished – it was about ten days – we tentatively made plans to see each other. Both of us were very conscious that we had our marriages and our kids. Even Dennis seemed to have a conscience about it. So we would meet somewhere on the A3 between Wimbledon and Richmond, drive up into a lay-by and sit in each other's cars but there was nothing more than holding hands and listening to music and wishing we were both freer, and I was in some turmoil because I was brought up as a Catholic to believe that marriage was forever and it was sacred. It wasn't something that I took the slightest bit lightly. I'd never been unfaithful to a long-standing partner before and never since.

My great close friend Krysia had a little flat in Chiswick, right up at the top of an old house, and I had the keys to this place. When we had a few hours we drove there separately and we would sit and listen to music and he would have a couple of drinks and we'd have a cuddle and talk about things. But we didn't really have any plans for it going on. It was a sort of liaison that hadn't developed into anything yet.

I was beginning to get bad-tempered at home and unable to explain why to my husband and the whole thing started to be difficult to cope with. I didn't know what I was going to do and I was sort of hoping it would fade out. But it wasn't fading, it was getting stronger. And there was that fascination all things have when they are forbidden and secret and dangerous. So after a while we started to talk about the possibility of getting together, although there was never any talk about us making it public. We were still keeping it secret. When I used to go and visit him on set there was an agreed codeword. I should have guessed this sort of thing had happened before, because everyone there was very adept at playing this game. I used to meet up with him whenever possible on the set and they all knew we were having a relationship. They had a codeword for me, 'Big Red' because of my hair. It was naive of me to think I was the first, or indeed the last. They may or may not have thought it was a full-blown thing but clearly we were seeing each other and they knew we had our partners and our families.

For eight months from summer 1981 Dennis was starring in the musical *Windy City* in the West End with Amanda Redman. It was a big production and there was a long rehearsal period. I wasn't around very much because I was on tour with a fairly dreadful play called *Mr Fothergill's Murder* but we spoke to each other every day, often several times. We were in that first incredibly excited phase when we desperately wanted to speak to and hear each other and write to each other. He wrote to me almost every day. I still have most of the letters he ever sent to me. He was a wonderful letter writer, incredibly romantic. Whenever he could, he would drive to whatever hotel or digs I was staying in and sometimes stay the night. How he explained this to his wife I'm not quite sure. I only did it when I was away.

I remember the first time I went to see a performance of *Windy City*, and I felt I was falling in love with Dennis all over again. He was an incredibly mesmeric performer and a wonderful singer but as always when you see someone you are crazy about acting love scenes with another woman, you feel a slight twinge of 'I wish that was me', although I knew I could never sing well enough to have a lead part in a stage musical of that calibre. During the months the show was running at the New Victoria I went often, not always to sit and watch but to visit him in his dressing room. I would go literally whenever I could get away or whenever I was in the West End. I used to be in his dressing room before, during, or after the show. It became known as the Waterman's Arms because he always had a well-stocked fridge of alcoholic beverages and the band and the crew used to come in and drink with him.

If there is rather more going on between a couple on stage than what's written in the script, you just know it. You have an intuition about these things, especially if you are close, and, I suppose, most especially if you're an actress yourself. I just sensed that there was something going on between Dennis and Amanda Redman. This was right at the beginning of us being really besotted with each other and when I questioned him about it he said, 'You're crazy. Why would I do something like that? We're just about hanging on to what we have at the moment, trying to make right decisions about us and the people that we're already married to and our families. Why would I jeopardise that? We have a romantic relationship in the show but that's literally all there is to it.'

A couple of times I found what I took to be slightly incriminating evidence, like a little locket on his dressing table which I think said 'Water under the Bridge'. That was the title of one of the numbers they had together. Unless you're involved with someone you don't give them things with personal messages like that. Amanda Redman was an attractive woman, she was very good in the musical and I'd already been warned about Dennis. He wasn't averse to flirting with women and he did have a reputation for being a bit of a ladies' man. I knew all those things.

He said I was being ridiculous about Amanda – he didn't have the time, he didn't have the energy and anyway why would he want to? I had serious doubts but I chose to believe him. He said, 'Why would I want hamburger when I've got steak?' It wasn't the last time I was to hear him say that. I'm not by nature a jealous or suspicious person, unless something is thrust under my nose, but I was suspicious about Amanda from the beginning and I turned out to be right.

Then one morning when I was at home with my husband Brian the phone rang. It was a journalist from a tabloid. Brian picked up the phone and they said, 'What truth is there in the story that your wife and Dennis Waterman are having a romantic liaison?'

Naturally, I knew this moment was going to come. We had been seeing each other for three months and it was always unlikely to remain a secret for long. I'm not sure if I'd planned what to do.

I told Brian there was no truth in it.

But as the days went by it got more and more difficult. Poor Brian was suffering from my lack of humour and my bad temper, and I didn't know what to do about the Dennis situation.

For a short time, a very short time, we talked about not seeing each other again, but the pull was just too powerful, so I admitted it to Brian. He is an extraordinary man, he's incredibly loyal and very kind and he said, 'Let's give it a few months and see if you can work it out of your system and let's not rush into anything rash.' He wouldn't stop me from seeing Dennis but he told me to think very carefully about what I was doing to us and in particular to our daughter. I stayed for about three months but it was impossible – I had to be with Dennis.

It was an almost exact echo of what happened when my mother fell in love with Nicky and went to tell my father about it. Brian and my father responded with the same great generosity and understanding and love and care for their children, maintaining an unbroken decades-long friendship with the wives who had left them. In that respect we were both very fortunate women.

Dennis had by this time already moved out of his family

home. So I had to face up to telling my parents and my family and friends, and then it was out in the open and the papers got hold of it and really ran with it because for its time it was a sort of Posh and Becks story. Dennis was probably the most famous and certainly the most loved of all British actors of his age and type – a star in two of the biggest shows on television – and I was well known for *Rock Follies* and, I am bound to say, we did indeed make a pretty good-looking couple.

We were by this time madly in love, or madly in something. In retrospect one wonders what love is actually based on. We didn't know an awful lot about each other but none of that seemed to be important because there was so much electricity and passion between us. If we didn't throw ourselves into it, life didn't seem worth living.

It was all very romantic. He was a superb singer and a great guitarist. And he would serenade me with all the big emotional love songs of the time. We were like kids. I don't think I ever remember a man telling me he loved me as often as Dennis used to – and he did it for several years to come.

On holiday with (from left) Lara, Julia, Dennis and Hannah Waterman.

CHAPTER 9

THIS IS GOING TO BE OUR NEST

We were both actors. We both had our careers, which at times would bring us together and at other times would be a source of friction. Being in love was really just about the only other thing we had in common. Socially, we were from different worlds – me with my background in the Polish nobility and with a strict Catholic upbringing, him the youngest of nine children of a working-class family in south London, who made his West End debut age thirteen. I was slightly hippyish and spiritually inclined with quite a strong tendency towards what we would now call new-age fads; and he, if not a full-blown hellraiser, was certainly very laddish. He loved sport – playing and watching – and much preferred socialising with men. And there was always drinking. I wasn't sporty, I wasn't laddish and I wasn't a drinker myself.

He drank a great deal and I saw this as a problem not just for me, though it would become a great strain. I also saw it as a problem for him. I always thought if he was loved more and taken care of more he would be stabilised and not feel the necessity to drink so much. I somehow believed that I would be able to love him and look after him better than anyone else. This was just female pride, stupid in many ways, not least because he had been loved. I knew that his previous wife had been a very good wife and a very good mother to their children. I think she had decided that Dennis was Dennis and, although he had been unfaithful to her more than once, she would accept him as he was. I was never quite able to do that.

We were looking for a house. One day he took me to Sheepcote, a hamlet in Buckinghamshire between Beaconsfield and Burnham Beeches, to look at a place. It wasn't grand but it was big and spacious and set in its own half-acre with a swimming pool and tennis court. The décor was pretty hideous but we would get over that. When we met the owners, I went into the kitchen with the woman while Dennis was taken off by the man and when they came back he said: 'That's it, this is definitely going to be our nest.' What had convinced him was the snooker room with its full-size snooker table. At the time I had no idea about the game. Apparently I walked into this huge room, saw this snooker table and said, 'What a great place for a party, can't we put that thing on wheels?' I didn't realise it weighed tons.

The house cost £150,000, which in 1982 was an enormous amount. We took out a huge mortgage but it was me who paid the deposit. My husband Brian was incredibly generous and gave me half the money from the sale of our house in Wimbledon. Dennis had no money whatsoever. He left the family home and everything in it with his wife and had nothing.

We were moving into a sizeable five-bedroom place and when we first got there we had just the few bits of furniture that I'd brought with me, about enough for one room. The first thing we went out to buy together was a bed. In the King's Road, at a beautiful shop called And So To Bed, we found one with a brass bedhead that was a sort of modern twisted lover's knot. Our romantic dream was becoming an everyday or every-night reality.

He was working and at that time I was working less because I wanted to get the house in order. We got a deal with a magazine. They would pay a certain amount towards redecoration in return for a long interview. So gradually the house was coming together. And I remember even in the early days waking up in the middle of the night and just wandering round and thinking, 'I just can't believe this is ours.'

One of the special things I used to arrange for Dennis and me on the few evenings when he was free was a candlelit dinner in front of the wood-burning stove in the snooker room – the whole room lit by candles and with our favourite music playing. We listened to the Eagles and the Byrds and especially Eric Clapton – 'Wonderful Tonight' was a top song with us then. As a present I gave Dennis a Fender Stratocaster that had belonged to Eric Clapton.

When Dennis was working early in the morning and needed to be picked up at six or six-thirty by his driver to go and do *Minder*, he would always leave a cup of tea by my bed, invariably with some adorable little note or love letter, and then occasionally when he had lie-ins in the morning, I would bring him a cup of tea.

My daughter Lara was living with us almost full time. His children used to come and visit very regularly at weekends and holidays. Dennis's daughter Julia was six months older than Lara, and Hannah was six years older than them.

One of the most precious times was weekends. Quite often Lara was away with her father and we had the house to ourselves. It was in the days before he became obsessed with golf, and it was just our time. Normally I would bring us breakfast in bed with the papers and we would have the *Sunday Times* and the *Mail on Sunday* and Dennis would go straight to the sports pages and I would start reading a bit of something in the *Mail*, and then the colour supplements, and we'd do crossword puzzles together in bed. And they were really special, those moments. There was nothing to interrupt or interfere. It was just the cosiness of us together in our gorgeous house. Until we realised how much it cost we were heating our outdoor swimming pool up to bath temperature and sitting in there and drinking champagne.

Dennis's youngest and my daughter became close friends. The times we spent at home when he wasn't working were just magical. I even pretended to be interested in football. I used to curl up with him on the sofa to watch *Match of the Day*, and serve him his vodka and tonic and be a housewife, looking after the kids and cooking meals.

Very soon after we moved into the house, we acquired a dog we named Silky after Enid Blyton's book *The Faraway Tree*. She was our first rescue animal and she was in a pretty bad state, mentally and physically. She quickly became the apple of both our eyes, and loved by the children. She was a cross between an Alsatian and a rough collie, a fairly extraordinary-looking amalgam of the two when we first got her, but she then blossomed into a really beautiful, highly intelligent animal and an important part of our lives. Very soon we started having charity rescue cats as well; altogether I think we had eight.

I'd always had dogs when I was growing up. I don't think Dennis ever had, but this animal life in the house was impor-tant to us, especially Silky. Even though I did most of the looking after Silky on a day-to-day basis, she was absolutely besotted with Dennis. Strangely enough, in later years when he used to come back from work late and things were not always so peachy, I could tell by the sound of the wheels on the gravel, or the way the key turned in the lock what sort of mood was coming home and Silky would know even before the car had come through the gate at the bottom of the driveway. I could tell from her body language whether things were going to be good, or not so good.

We had fantastic evenings at home playing Scrabble and Boggle and snooker. And snooker quickly became a favourite, because I was able to beat Dennis's mates when they got plastered. I was still sober and learning the game and beginning to love it. There were amazing evenings. I remember Steve Davis came to give us snooker lessons. I had what he thought was a natural ability to pot the ball, though when it came to learning how to manoeuvre the white ball for the next shot everything went out of the window.

We went on having good lessons and Hurricane Higgins came over one evening. Warren Clarke, who is now very well known for *Dalziel and Pascoe* and many other things, was very close to Dennis and he and his wife Michèle (one of my best friends to this day) were regular visitors. And the Walfords, whose place Dennis had stayed at when we first begun our affair, used to visit and, oh, many of our friends and my family. Almost every week there was some huge get-together with family meals and picnics, and swimming pool, tennis courts and a barbecue.

We had friends we stayed with in south-east France and while we were there we bought a wreck of a house with some land on a hillside at Vidauban in the Var. It was more or less a ruin but we were very much in love and we had wonderful plans for it. A couple of years later, work did actually start on it, though it remained very far from ever being completed. I spoke good French and loved the idea of one day perhaps becoming part of the community there, though Dennis wasn't quite so hooked on the idea. Learning a different language really didn't appeal to him at all.

We lived a charmed life. Whenever he went touring with his charity football team, which was often, I used to drag the kids out to pitches all over the country in the mud and the rain and the snow and sit there signing autographs and looking after them while he played with the lads. We were blissfully happy when we were at home together but perhaps I was trying too hard to be one of the boys. I suppose I felt I had to do that to be part of his world. I didn't enjoy it much and on reflection I don't think he did either. Then there were lots of things in my life that he didn't share. I was keener on travelling to exotic places than he was and he wasn't as interested in doing crazy intrepid things as me, though he did learn to love travelling together. We went to Rarotonga, a coral atoll in the Pacific; to

St Lucia; to China on a fantastic three-week trip; to Tomberua, an island off the coast of Fiji billed as romantic and enchanting – 'four acres of pristine coral reef with ten traditionally designed cottages in the middle of the ocean' – for a less than perfect stay. At high tide it was as described, though the cottages were so close together you could hear your neighbours brushing their teeth, but at low tide it was twice the size, with no shade, and the sea was full of poisonous snakes.

For a short time I took up hot-air ballooning. It started with a charity stunt for Children with Leukaemia, which we were both quite deeply involved with, and there were fun photographs sold to raise money. Then it was mooted that it would be a good idea if I trained to become a pilot, which I did. One of the other reasons for doing that was my fear of flying, which it did really help with, but it's a pretty antisocial sport timing-wise because you either fly at the crack of dawn or in the very early hours of the evening, when there are no thermal winds.

At first Dennis was quite interested in that and the kids were thrilled with it, and he would travel in the retrieve car to pick the balloon up. But then he got a bit bored, which was understandable, because you're not really part of the whole balloon thing unless you are flying it. And I had many other enthusiasms, often quite airy-fairy, that came and went and certainly didn't appeal to him. And he definitely wasn't interested in Buddhism, which really became important to me. He didn't have any spiritual beliefs or any spiritual leanings at all.

Dennis was trying very hard to be a family man. He was very good at kissing and cuddling and telling off, but he was not good at spending time with the children and he wasn't terribly interested in their development. As far as that was concerned he seemed quite Victorian in his attitudes. The children, when they stayed with us, for either a weekend or longer, played acting games. Clearly they – particularly his two – had the acting gene in them. We used to have a huge dressing-up box and the kids would compose little plays and then we had to go into the nursery to watch them. Dennis was quite indulgent when they were younger, but he was not – and I think he would admit it himself – a person who found family life on a regular basis an easy thing to do. It didn't come naturally to him at all.

Yes, he would occasionally read stories to the kids, but he was not a great father figure, though in the first few years he did try, and I was aware of that and I was very grateful for it.

There were times even in those early years when we'd got all the children together for the weekend and there would be arguments about what should take priority. Should we try and make a family day for them as I wanted or should he go off and do four or five hours in the boozer? And I would ask, what's the point of having the kids for the weekend if you're not going to see them? There were slight sadnesses about moments like that and there were times when other friends of mine used to come with their kids and all the blokes would go off to the pub together and the women would stay in the house.

Then the men would come back, mostly gently oiled, and the afternoon or the evening would disintegrate around the snooker room, which became the hub for many a party – and of course in the summer months we had the swimming pool, so the kids would all be up there with us ladies while the blokes would be getting drunker. And then when the children went to bed, we'd all carry on partying. Mostly they were wonderful times but occasionally the behaviour of the men, when they'd had quite a lot to drink, became 'inelegant', for want of a better word.

It was a perfect house for parties, for weekends and for when my sister used to come over from America with her family. Obviously it was wonderful for both my parents because it was within easy striking distance of London and the big family occasions, like Christmas, Easter and birthdays, always so beautiful. I did the traditional Polish Christmas, which was on Christmas Eve, and we would have both my mother and my father – even though they were no longer together – and my father's lady friend, Tania. They were all the greatest of friends. And my sisters and my brother would come – Anna,

Gaba with her husband Robert, and children Marc and Izzie, and Andrew with his wife Jacqui and their kids Toby and Otto, and even my stepfather's children with their families, and Dennis's family, when they were over from America.

Dennis was always hugely generous with his gifts and they were just magical, wonderful times. My family have lots of traditions we keep up and I think Dennis found the whole thing a little difficult to come to terms with in the beginning. For a start, a lot of it was very Polish and anyway I don't think tradition and customs – in that way – had played much part in his life, certainly not an important part, whereas for me, because of my background, because my parents were Polish, all these things had been very deeply instilled and they were essential.

One of the most charming was on our birthdays. My mother always used to decorate our chair with flowers, the breakfast chair, and balloons and greenery and cards and presents would be laid out on the breakfast table – and this is something I brought into our life, which he got to like in the end.

Obviously, the fact that I'd taken my daughter away from her father always weighed fairly heavily on my conscience and Brian was always there during her childhood on a regular basis and she would go for weekends to him. He was never judgemental. He was never antagonistic. He accepted things for how they were and his relationship with his daughter never suffered. But the discomfort I felt, having taken her away from somebody who was an incredibly hands-on father, was sometimes difficult.

I got the impression that Dennis's children, going backwards and forwards to and from their mother, never really suffered as much when they were separated from their father as my daughter did when she was separated from hers. But they had a great relationship with each other, the children, and I thought I had a great relationship with them. I tried to be as fair as possible and to remember that as a stepmother you can't actually be a mother as such, that wasn't my place. But while they were in our house with us, there were certain rules we had to make as a family that obviously might have been slightly different from the rules they had when they were living with their mother.

The relationships between Dennis and his ex-wife Pat and her new husband (whom she married fairly quickly after Dennis and she split) – and my relationship with my first husband – were all good and there was never any discomfort when they either delivered or picked up the children, occasionally staying for dinner or another meal. It was quite a relaxed, easy atmosphere. And I really thought I had a very good friendship with his children and I loved them, although they had their problems. And because Dennis was not the sort of person who remembered things like birthdays or Christmas presents, I took care of that as any woman who runs a household would.

When everything started falling apart years later, it was incredibly hurtful to see bits in newspapers that his children had supposedly written about me. I found it completely incomprehensible. Suddenly, I had become the wicked stepmother from hell. And although it's completely understandable that they would defend their father – blood is thicker than water – on more than one occasion they were certainly present to witness his mental unpleasantness towards me when he was seriously drunk. The children were there. They saw it, they heard it. But I suppose they were far too young to understand, let alone take part, thank God.

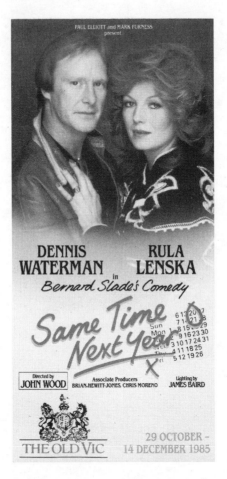

What a joy acting in this beautiful play and being deeply in love.
(© Brian Aris)

CHAPTER 10

LIVING TOGETHER, WORKING TOGETHER

Dennis really felt a woman's place was in the home, looking after her man and dealing with the house. When we met I had my own career, not nearly as stellar as his but really pretty successful in my own way. He often reminded me later, and would certainly tell other people, that the major part of the mortgage and other things were paid by him. They certainly were; he was earning an enormous amount.

He kept telling me I didn't need to work any more, he earned enough for the both of us and I should concentrate on being at home with the children. But I always needed the career. Much as I loved being at home, I loved acting too. Somehow if I wasn't doing the work I had been trained for I felt half empty.

We were lucky to have nannies to look after Lara and to share taking her to the local school in Gerrards Cross. I was still doing quite a lot of touring and making the odd television guest appearance in things like *Doctor Who*, *Robin of Sherwood*, *The Brothers*, *Casualty*, *The Detectives*, *Minder* and quiz shows – *Blankety Blank* and *Call My Bluff*. A lot of those bits of work were just sort of celebrity appearances, which I wasn't very keen on, and the money wasn't brilliant either but there was a lot of pleasure. I was in the *Morecambe and Wise* Christmas television show, which was a joy. And when you are asked to do *Blankety Blank* with Les Dawson, how can you say no? In those days it was considered quite a good thing to do, just to keep your face out there.

Dennis was not very keen on theatre because the discipline required meant he couldn't go off for his regular bevvies with his mates. Television was much better for that. But we started to be offered really good theatre work together and for me this was a dream.

In 1985 we did *Same Time Next Year*, a play that had already been made into a very successful film with Alan Alda and Ellen Burstyn. It's about a couple, both married to other people, who meet by chance in a hotel in America. They fall in love and agree to get together every year, but the play only sees them every five years or so. And so there are five episodes and we see the physical change, from an 18-year-old girl to a 24-year-old, to a 30-year-old woman and it goes on until they're in their sixties or seventies. Very funny, very touching.

It opened at the Old Vic and then toured all over the country. We got fantastic reviews and we did a sort of pre-publicity tour. We were flown to some places by helicopter and taken to others in chauffeur-driven cars. It was great fun. We were very popular with the press and the public, everybody wanted interviews and photographs and autographs and Dennis was very good-tempered about doing that sort of stuff. We were living together, working together, earning together – we were with each other 24/7. We absolutely loved it. I couldn't think of anything more wonderful.

There were occasional hiccups because of the drinking and because, by his own admission, he did like the company of men more than the company of women. He always enjoyed having a woman on his arm but when it came to actual conversation, he preferred men. Anyway, we had huge success with the play and then it was suggested we take it to Australia and New Zealand, so we said yes – as long as we could take the children with us for part of the time.

For some actors' union reason or other we weren't allowed to play anywhere in Australia except Perth, where we were on for a month. So we hired this wonderful apartment which, oddly enough, was called Minderup and we had the kids with us and a nanny called Jean, who was terrific, and we were playing to packed houses every night with people queuing round the block for returns. For me it was a time of great joy and excitement. I was doing something I loved with someone I loved, and the audiences, the general public and the press adored us. And we were having amazing adventures.

We took the children swimming with dolphins and to all sorts of extraordinary places, we cuddled koalas and kangaroos. And sometimes between the matinée and the evening show we would scoot back to the apartment when the kids were out with the nanny and go to bed for a siesta. Those really were glorious times.

We were hassled quite a lot on the street. At that time we really enjoyed the attention but Dennis became less and less keen on public intervention later on. Anyway, the best of all was to get away by ourselves, though this wasn't always easy. I remember one weekend we were invited to a barbecue somewhere quite a long way out of the centre of Perth, and we thought we were the only people there. The kids were playing in the woods; I suddenly felt the call of nature and went off to find a suitable tree and I was just squatting down with my knickers round my ankles when this little head popped up from behind a neighbouring tree and said, 'G'day, could I have your autograph please?' My reply was, 'I'm so sorry, I haven't got a pencil.'

In Australia Dennis was very much in his element because the men and the women weren't really integrated, and they still aren't, not like they are over here. Dennis was huge there; *Minder* was enormous. *Rock Follies* was big too: the series had been repeated at least three times and the album went platinum. Even so, people would come up and say, 'Dennis, how great to see you', totally ignoring me. And Dennis would say, 'and this is my girlfriend, Rula', and they would say, 'Oh, hi' and stand in front of me and continue the conversation with Dennis. Naturally, I found this very irksome but in those days Dennis was protective and he would draw me back into the conversation.

We were very physical in public, always touching and holding hands, arms round each other, and we were very close with the children. We involved them in everything and they had an extraordinary time. Then they had to go back to England, back to school, and we had another month of touring New Zealand – North and South Island.

We played to packed houses there, too. New Zealand died at half past nine or ten o'clock in the evening. There was absolutely nothing to do. Once we had finished we just went back to our little place, sometimes a hotel, sometimes a cottage we had rented, and we were perfectly happy. We would watch films or just cuddle up in bed.

Every day was a new adventure. We went out a lot when we were in Wellington. We were taken to a stud farm where we were actually forced to watch these incredibly expensive stallions mounting mares. We flew up to Mount Cook. One of my favourite places was Rotorua, with its geysers and hot bubbling mud pools. Everyone said to us that within two or three days you get accustomed to the rotten-eggs smell of hydrogen sulphide – true? Possibly. We drove down a huge motorway that goes for miles and miles along the Kaikoura coast. There didn't seem to be any other cars or people, just loads of sheep. You're right next to the beach. We stopped and bought ourselves half a crayfish and sat right in the middle of a seal colony – just the two of us.

Actually, it isn't quite true to say we were together all the time when we were in plays together. Being the diligent stage actress, I liked to be in the theatre at least an hour before the show, to get into character. It was a holy sort of meditative time in the dressing room. Dennis would go out drinking and arrive five minutes before curtain-up.

There were a few times on stage during *Same Time Next Year* when that made itself felt. Of course, knowing Dennis, I wasn't surprised. On one occasion he forgot my character's name, which was Doris. The first scene opens with us scrambling out of bed, me getting dressed under the covers, and I remember he said to me something like, 'Glenys, Dw... whatever the fuck your name is...' This was all in an American accent. The audience thought it was hysterically funny and all part of the script. Even when he was a bit pissed he was always able to carry on and always able to ad lib. But sometimes it did scare me.

There was a piano on the set, three-quarters facing the audience so they couldn't see the keyboard. And, I think it was in the third scene, it's my birthday and I came in dressed as a sort of Marilyn Monroe character in a blonde wig – with a very full 1950s skirt – and he starts to play the 'Moonlight' Sonata.

It was pre-recorded but he used to mime it amazingly well and nobody believed he wasn't playing it. So he lifted up his hands, which was the cue, and he put them down on the keys and nothing happened. So he did it again. Nothing happened. Then he got up and walked away and the piano started to play. So he kicked the piano and said, 'Fuck. Japanese shit.' It brought the house down.

He could handle it but I'm a terrible corpser on stage. Once I start to giggle, that's it. In one of the scenes towards the end of the play, the curtain goes up as we're both supposedly in bed after a night of passion, and because the curtain never comes down we had to get into our places in a blackout, having changed wigs and hairpieces and so on. I was in between the sheets, as I should have been, and he was under the bottom sheet, which for some reason I found hilariously funny. I just could not get my lines out and there were tears pouring down my face, until he dug me in the ribs and said, 'Doris, pull yourself together.'

When we came back after our month in New Zealand we were even more in love, full of our adventures and longing to share them with friends and family and show photographs. And then he went off to do some more telly and I went off to do a very good two-hander, *Conversations with a Stranger* with John Stride, also for television, and I remember he used to turn up with the most extraordinary surprises. He was a very, very generous man, financially. One day he came with these two big boxes, one with a stunning three-quarter length leather jacket and the other a Yamamoto embroidered jacket – extremely expensive and for no particular reason. And, as I said, he used to write the most beautiful romantic letters, which I still have. Later I found out that some of the phrases I thought were completely unique were also used on his other lovers.

Two years after the delights of *Same Time Next Year*, we were going to Australia again to play together in Tom Stoppard's *The Real Thing*. Perhaps inspired by that title, we decided to get married. We had been together for more than five years and it seemed like an omen – the real thing. We hoped it might confer its own special blessing on us.

My mother came out to Perth for the wedding with the three children and Kathy, the nanny. Paul Elliott, who was the producer of the play, did most of the organising. He found this couple with a beautiful house and they made the tennis court into a sort of wedding pavilion garlanded with flowers and candles, and even the swimming pool was full of floating tea lights. Knowing how hot it was going to be out there I'd had a silk kaftan made in England – just white silk with tiny seed pearls; the girls had little smock dresses and Dennis was in white trousers and a white shirt and we were all barefoot. It was beautiful. Everything was decorated with twinkly lights and I had lots of little flowers in my hair.

We invited Brian Aris, a friend of ours who is a top celebrity photographer. He came out with his lady, who was part Polish, to do the official wedding photographs. I remember, months later, looking at the pictures and seeing Lara's little woebegone face, not at all happy at the ceremony. Unlike Dennis's daughters she never liked being photographed, and later I found out that one of the main reasons for her unhappiness was that in the marriage vows it said, 'For better, for worse, and wherever you go she shall follow,' or words to that effect. So Lara in her little head translated it as me being away from her again, not realising that we were talking about the family being bound together not torn apart.

The wedding was extremely beautiful but Dennis got very, very, very drunk. And on the morning of the wedding we got a telegram from his brother, which said, 'Congratulations on your wedding. PS Our father died this morning.' And I remember my mother thinking, 'How could he possibly put those two things into the same telegram?', but Dennis thought it was quite funny – he and his father had never had much of a relationship. I didn't even know his father was alive until our second year together.

For our wedding night we had been given a very sprauncy hotel suite, replete, I remember, with delicious baked goodies and things, all with our names iced on. Just the one night off from the play. And then, for the weekend, it had been organised for us, the girls, my mother and Brian Aris all to fly out in two tiny planes to a place called Monkey Mia, where wild dolphins come in from the sea to spend time with human beings – through their own choice, unlured there by food or anything like that.

We arrived at this extraordinary place, walked down to the sea and stood waist-deep in the water with these dolphins which just appeared out of nowhere with their babies, swimming round our legs. And I have a picture of my mother with tears pouring down her face. She just couldn't believe where she was and what she was doing. The following day we were back on stage.

But there was still more wedding to come. It was to be held in Queens Park, in the centre of Perth, in February in about 42 degrees and this was a traditional Aboriginal ceremony, their way of celebrating the fact that we were getting married in Australia. We would be made official holders of a certain amount of wetlands around the area. And David Gulpilil (from the film *Walkabout*) was there with his own musical group of Aboriginals. I'm sure you know Aboriginal music but it isn't the most exciting as far as musical content goes; it's rhythmic with a lot of didgeridoo and strange chanting.

We were led into this clearing and Dennis was made up as the white eagle, stripped to the waist, and I was the black crow, which I thought was a strange portent of inequality. Then we were led, holding each other by our little fingers, up into the main area of the park. There were a lot of people watching.

Dennis was sent off with the boys and I was sent off with the women and there were hours of posturing and screaming and shouting and I just sat amongst this group of women, thinking that they didn't speak any English whatsoever. It was swelteringly hot and at one point I turned to one of these women, thinking I ought to make some sort of conversation. I was trying in pidgin English to say something when she turned around to me and said, 'It's fucking hot, isn't it?'

After the ceremony we were taken by one of the chief Aborigines into the dream caves, a part of their religious belief that I found a great deal more fascinating than Dennis did, though he enjoyed the whole ceremony thing and the fact that we'd been officially made guardians of these wetlands. He was given a ceremonial didgeridoo and I was given a digging stick and we had to go and do a few pseudo-Aboriginal activities like chewing on a witchetty grub so that we could be enrolled for our duties of guardianship. And I remember wondering later, when the whole marriage fell apart, what happened to our duties over there now? I wonder if the Aborigines ever found out.

We were there for about six weeks. The America's Cup was being held out of Fremantle in Perth at the time. And we met Colonel John Blashford-Snell, the great explorer and originator of Operation Drake and Operation Raleigh. Thanks to Dennis's generosity it eventually turned out to be a fruitful meeting for me.

One of my adopted elephants, Burra, in Tsavo.

CHAPTER 11

THE THING ABOUT ELEPHANTS

Dennis was brilliant with ideas and presents in those days. For our first wedding anniversary he had arranged a trip to Venice. We travelled there from Paris on the *Orient Express*, which I had organised, and I can't think of anything much more romantic. It was one of the places that I'd always dreamed of going to. And I remember when we arrived in the early evening all the lights were twinkling. It wasn't the best part of the year – it was February – but it was so beautiful and here we were, the two of us, together on our first anniversary in this place my mother had always told me so much about. I just started crying uncontrollably, and I'll never forget Dennis turning to me and saying, 'What the bloody hell are you crying about?' and I said, 'It's so romantic, it's so beautiful, it's so amazing that the two of us are here together on such a special occasion,' and he said, 'Oh, pull yourself together.'

He couldn't understand the sort of romance that had been bred into me since childhood – sights and sounds and smells and nostalgia and all of those things were very much part of my make-up but not really part of his. And then, as luck would have it, he got the most horrendous attack of gout for the four days we were in Venice, so he didn't do an awful lot of sightseeing. He was laid up in agony in his hotel bed. That's what you call bad timing.

Six years later, things in our life were rather different – Dennis had returned after the hiatus I describe in the next chapter. Our marriage now was certainly a bit rocky, but for our seventh anniversary he truly excelled himself, though this time it was something for me to do by myself, not us two together. I knew something very special was being planned because my daughter Lara and my sister Anna kept dropping very intriguing hints … 'Oh, Mama you will never believe this,' and 'Oh my God, you are so lucky.'

Dennis and Lara brought me breakfast in bed and on the tray was a large, thick envelope. Sipping my tea, I opened it and the words that met my eyes were 'Discovery Expeditions … giant elephant quest … with Colonel Blashford-Snell'. We had met him in Perth and Dennis of course knew that for me going on something like this would be a dream come true.

There was a brochure and itinerary and a detailed letter outlining the most incredible expedition to India and Nepal: his second attempt to find two giant elephants which had been spotted on previous trips. I was absolutely speechless.

Six weeks to go, to prepare for this most magical of

adventures. It was to be a proper working expedition with experts in different fields including Adrian Lister, an eminent palaeontologist, Pat Troy, a former major in the Royal Marines, Wendy Bentall, an expert on botany, an adventurous doctor called Michael Wilson, Paula Urschell, a delightful nurse from California, and, of course, Blashers – everyone calls him Blashers, though on the trip I took to calling him Lion and he called me Tigress, and so it has remained ever since.

There were endless jabs and special kit and cameras to sort out and books to read. We were all to have specific duties and one of mine was to take photographs and keep a daily diary. I was no expert with a camera but I was a keen amateur and determined that if we did manage to come across the legendary giants I would get the best photo ever. We did in fact also have a professional photographer with us from *Hello!* magazine, but I was adamant I did not want glossy posed glamour jungle photos; they had to be in keeping with the situation and in working clothes. As it turned out he kept a wonderful record of the whole trip and did some smashing snaps of me.

We flew to Delhi and were lucky enough to get upgraded – all fifteen of us – which is of course a huge comfort on a long-haul flight. Then there was a ten-hour bone-shattering coach drive to Corbett National Park. Amazing sights of Indian daily life took one's mind off the discomfort: the smell, the noise, the animals, the colourful sari-clad women and the millions of bikes and rickshaws were all a first for me.

We finally arrived at a rather grim-looking place laughably named Quality Inn Lodge and we were assigned our room partners for the few nights we were to spend there. Though hot and steamy during the day, at night the temperatures plummeted, and after a meal I crashed fully clothed and covered myself with whatever was available on our incredibly hard and uncomfortable beds.

Up at 4 a.m., we set off on our first game drive and to meet the elephants we would be riding through the park. We had two experienced Nepali naturalists who would be with us throughout the trip, Dhan Bahadur and Ram Din, both of whom I have met several times since and both of whom have remained special friends. A few years later when I went back to Nepal to do a short travel film for the BBC I asked for Dhan and Ram Din for the filming when I was in Chitwan, and they were both there. It was a very happy and tearful reunion.

The first few days in Corbett were disappointing. No wildlife at all, although we were shown a very furious leopard that had got caught in some wire fencing and was being driven further away to be released. But just being on the elephants and learning from Dhan and Ram Din about their experiences was a lesson each day, though it was sad not to see anything at all in the way of wildlife. So we were all looking forward to the next stage of the journey: a visit to the legendary Billy Arjan Singh, who lived on the Indo-Nepalese border. He was the only person ever to have hand-reared both a leopard and a tigress and successfully released them back into the wild.

The journey should have taken about seven hours but it ended up taking twice as long and as we approached in the total darkness to the edge of the park boundaries the driver drove us straight into a flooded river. We were well and truly stuck. I was longing for adventure even though we were all exhausted. We lit some small fires, because theoretically there were wild elephants, tigers and rhinos in the area, not to mention hordes of very persistent mosquitos. Finally Dhan decided to jog to the park gates for some help. I was not allowed to go with him. Soon he was back with Mr Khan, pink-teethed and reeking of heavily perfumed betel nut. And we were all shuttled to the lodge and shown to our mixed dormitories. Moth-eaten mattresses and blankets were moved close together, as once again it was freezing, and within half an hour everyone put together their stashes of alcohol and we were all giggling like school kids as we tried to grab a few hours' sleep.

Another foggy cold and animal-less safari the following morning depressed me further. It seemed incredible, with all the promises of the park being filled with wildlife, that nothing but barasingha deer and the odd bird made themselves visible. It was so different from Africa, where you were almost always guaranteed to see big game on every safari outing. Finally a tractor was found to rescue our poor bus and our luggage, and after hours of us all pushing and cajoling the bus out of the mud we were taken to Billy's cosy lodge.

Here, joy of joys, we had an old-fashioned tin bath filled with piping hot water carefully carried in by smiling house boys. And although you had to be a bit of a contortionist it was a joy and a luxury after several days with no proper washing to have clean hair and body. Then we had delicious home-cooked curry and watched the films of Tara the tiger cub and Harriet the leopard that Billy had raised and released. But, again, during the few days we were there we saw very little in the way of wildlife and I was beginning to become very despondent, just hoping and praying that our final destination would produce results.

We set off on the last leg of the journey to Bardia, the ex-royal Nepalese private hunting ground where the two huge elephants had been sighted a few years previously and an area which was also supposedly rich with tiger, rhino and wild elephant.

I will never forget the first sight of our own little tented camp where we would be for about ten days; individual tents in shades of faded brown against a pink sky and flanked by a riverbank. Each tent had its own bamboo stand with a plastic bowl and bucket. We were surrounded by softly scented rosewood and acacia trees and the smoke from the campfire drifted deliciously around us. Our elephant camp was about a minute's walk from our tents so I immediately went to with

Dhan to meet the elephants who were going to be working with us during our time there.

There were five of them. Madu Mala Kali was the oldest and the matriarch. Blashers nicknamed her Honey Blossom. Then there was Lakshmi Kali, named after the goddess of wealth; Sundar Kali, meaning beautiful; Champa Kali, meaning flower; and finally the youngest and cheekiest, Chan Chan Kali, who was to become my favourite. The sun was going down, the sound of the tree frogs was deafening and I was in heaven.

We had a wonderful meal, then Blashers warned us to make sure to check our boots for scorpions and reminded us that there was no fencing round the camp and if we needed to get up to go to the loo in the night to be careful not only about snakes but about some of the big game which might come wandering into the camp out of curiosity.

The drumming of the mahouts in the elephant camp next door and the ambient sound of the jungle was soporific. As soon as my head hit the pillow I was out like a light and dreaming of tigers and giant elephants. The following days were magical. We found the giant elephants, and what an amazing sight they were. We took many photos, dung samples and measurements from the footprints and followed them for several hours.

Every hour was filled with sightings and experiences and magic, though sadly we never saw a tiger, much as we'd longed to. Each day saw us up at dawn and on our highly trained

and beautiful lady elephants for several hours before returning to camp for a wonderful brunch and writing up of notes.
Each evening while the rest of the group would sit around
the campfire drinking from the incredibly well-stocked jungle
bar I would sneak off to the elephant camp with Dhan and
sit with the elephants as their keepers endlessly made special
elephant sandwiches and drummed into the small hours of
the morning.

Watched by the elephants gently swaying to the rhythms,
I would sit near Chan Chan Kali and her trunk would sometimes gently wind itself round my shoulders as she rumbled
and blew soft breath on to my head. It was a very humbling
experience to be so close to the largest and most intelligent of
all land mammals, in trust and without fear.

Sometimes we would hear what Dhan said were tigers making
love in the distance – a deep, throaty 'vrooooooooooooooom'.
It was almost incredible to feel that here I was, totally unpro-
tected in a place where humans were not the rulers. No phones,
no intruding technology. Just hurricane lamps and the sounds
and smells of the jungle. Very special. I don't think I have ever
slept so well.

Every evening the elephants would be checked to see
whether they had any thorns in their feet. They understood
between forty and fifty verbal commands, sometimes really
intricate ones. On this particular evening we discovered that
Chan Chan Kali, my favourite, had a two-inch-long bamboo

thorn embedded in her front foot. She lay good as gold, with me stroking her head, while one of the phanits, the men who looked after the elephants, sang to her as we dug out the offending thorn. This was obviously painful. You could see her huge body shuddering with the penknife going deeper and deeper. Finally we managed to extract it with a pair of my tweezers. This was all under hurricane lamps. We poured boiling-hot disinfectant into the wound, which must have been agony. Shortly afterwards she was given the command to stand. She gently tried out the weight on her foot and then slowly twined her trunk around my neck as if to say thank you.

Jack, our photographer, had to get some photos for *Hello!* magazine. To my delight he decided a shot with an elephant would be the best option. The phanits made mounting look so simple. The elephant would lift a front foot and the phanit used it as an elevator to ear level, then he would grab the ears and swivel himself round to sit astride the elephants neck. It's not as easy as it looks. We tried it twice. The photographer wanted to get one with the Himalayas in the background. The first time the light was wrong, the second time I wasn't look-ing at the camera, and as we were going for the third attempt Dhan said, 'You better get it right this time otherwise she may get bored and just toss Rula right over her back!' Luckily, we got our shot.

All too soon this idyllic short stay in the jungle had to come to an end. We travelled back laden with photographs and dung samples and measurements and diaries filled with facts and botanical specimens, our hearts and souls filled with wonderful memories and already planning a return visit the following year.

The giggles, the hardships, the wonder and sometimes the pain – but this truly was the best present I had ever had. Thank you, Dennis ... a thousand 'namastes', the traditional Nepali greeting that means 'blessings to the god within you'.

CHAPTER 12

'EITHER HER OR ME'

The first time I found out Dennis was being unfaithful there had been no previous outward signs at all. In the very early days, of course, there was Amanda Redman, but for the previous eight or nine years I had never had any reason to suspect. If there had been reason, I didn't know about it. He'd gone out to Portugal to do some filming for his television comedy drama series *Stay Lucky*, and I used to pack his suitcases for him and unpack them again, because he couldn't be bothered. And he had just come back, with beautiful presents and perfume. We had spoken every evening on the phone and he had been very loving and warm, as he always was.

He had taken his suitcases upstairs; he had also taken his briefcase up and somehow it undid itself and sort of opened and I noticed these two sheets of paper had come away from his notebook and fallen on to the floor. I casually picked them up and I saw a love letter from this woman, 'My beloved, how am I ever going to live without you? These last two weeks have been more than I could ever have dreamed,' blah, blah, blah. So, shaking with fury and complete disbelief, I took this letter down and confronted Dennis with it and he said, 'Oh, it's really nothing. It was just a tiny fling and I'm so sorry.' And he used the words he had used when he lied about his relationship with Amanda Redman: 'How could I possibly want hamburger, when I've got the best steak in the world at home?'

On another occasion – he wasn't very good at hiding things or putting things away – he had left stuff lying around and I found a letter from him to his lover Fiona. He had used the phrases which I thought so adorable, and personal and unique and romantic, when he wrote them to me: 'I can't wait to walk down the street holding hands and shouting my love to you, to the world' and 'I can't wait to wake up with your hair spread on the pillow next to me'. Now here they were again, addressed to somebody else – exactly the same words – it really, really hurt.

He promised me that it was over, and life sort of went on, but several months later when he was rehearsing in London I did something that I didn't very often do. I rang the rehearsal room. The PA answered the phone and I said, 'Could I speak to Dennis please?' and without even asking who it was, the woman said, 'Oh, hi Fiona, I'll get him for you.'

And that was it. I saw red and I said to him: 'You promised me it was finished. You decide now. Either her or me and get out while you're deciding.' That's when the mistrust really set in and never properly healed. Every time he went away after that I was very nervous and worried that it was carrying on. And I also know that it did carry on, and that he was carefully protected by his agent, by his drivers, by his stand-ins, by the production company. Everybody knew they were now protecting him and her in the same way they had protected him and me.

He was commuting backwards and forwards to Leeds filming *Stay Lucky*. So he would be in Leeds during the week. I knew she was a production assistant on the programme, so I think anybody would have stayed scared that this wasn't finished. But he brought me back beautiful presents and he said, 'You know what it's like, you have a gentle flirt when you're on location, but it really doesn't mean anything,' and I was willing to be convinced that it was nothing more.

He was very solicitous and warm and loving and caring, but when that seed of suspicion is sown it's very hard to get rid of it, particularly when he's going back to the scene of the crime on a regular basis. I think he once told me she had been moved on to another programme, or she had lost her position or something like that, to try to reassure me and he said I was welcome to go up to Leeds whenever I wanted to, but trust had disappeared long before that.

We were in serious money trouble. He had borrowed a lot of money to finance a film and he put up the house, including my part of the house (because it was in joint names), as collateral. The film was originally called *Father Jim* – later changed to *Cold Justice* – and he was making it in Chicago with Roger Daltrey of The Who. I knew he was risking some of his own money but I didn't realise that he was putting up the whole of the house, including my half.

He went off to Chicago to do the movie and I went out there to visit him; the premise of the film was quite good and the script seemed okay too. It was all a bit of a cliquey group – the producer and the director were friends of Dennis's. I don't know how much money was borrowed from other sources, whether Dennis actually borrowed from his agents, or from other people he knew. But when the film crashed people started demanding their money back. It was a terrible crisis for all of us and there was no escape from it, but Dennis always liked to duck trouble. He would rather get drunk than deal with difficult situations. He tried to explain to me, at one point, one of the things he liked about Fiona: 'I don't have to explain myself to her.' I said, 'Well, of course you don't have to explain yourself to her, you don't have a family with her and you don't share a house together.'

He was offered the chance to go back to Australia to do *Jeffrey Bernard Is Unwell*, the brilliantly funny play about the real-life magazine columnist and Soho drinker, a part that fitted him like a glove. But rather than going out there on his own and really thinking about things and sorting his life out, blow me down, he takes Fiona with him. He didn't tell me but I found out fairly soon. It was like the end of my life. How am

I going to survive? What's going to happen to me? What's going to happen to my daughter? What's going to happen to my stepchildren? How is this all going to be resolved? I thought it was incredibly cowardly of him. He said he just couldn't stand being accused any more of having landed us in really serious trouble financially, quite apart from everything else he'd done.

My daughter Lara was thirteen years old. She was an only child. It was hard to find a nanny who was interested in looking after a girl of that age and it would be expensive. I had to work, and contact with Dennis's children had been more or less severed when he went off to Australia. I had been very determined that I would never send Lara away to school because I hadn't been happy boarding but it now became a necessary option. At least she would have the daily companionship of children her own age and she wouldn't be around to see her mother falling to pieces. I honestly didn't know what was going to happen but I didn't want her to be here, in case things got really unpleasant. So at the time it seemed a good thing to do. Thank God her father helped with school fees.

I was very hurt and there was so much to cope with. I was desperately worried that we would have to leave the house because of all the money we owed. And I had to find a way of coping with the situation. After six months I was in a state of collapse. If it wasn't a fully fledged nervous breakdown it was close to it. I was going for regular counselling, I was taking

antidepressant drugs. My family were, as always, amazing –
incredibly supportive – particularly my youngest sister, Anna.

Warren and Michèle Clarke were very important to me.
Warren had been a close friend of Dennis for a long time, even
before I was on the scene. But Michèle was my special friend
and we saw each other on a virtually daily basis throughout all
the time I was in Sheepcote, and she was extremely kind and
helpful, though for her, married to an old friend of Dennis, it
was a difficult situation. But when Dennis ran off to Australia
he didn't just run off from me, he ran off from everybody.
Michèle felt that too. She was always insistent that if ever I
needed help, if I ever needed advice, she was there to give it.

By far the happiest day of that unhappy year was my mother's seventieth birthday. It was in the middle of the summer
and the house was at its best. Relatives came from far and
wide: her brothers, one from Dublin and one from Munich,
with their spouses and their children; my sister Gaba from
America with her two children; and of course my father,
because, though long separated, my parents had remained
the best of friends. There were about forty or forty-five of us.
Dennis wasn't around, of course.

I collected Mama from London. She thought she was just
coming for lunch with me. I drove up through the gates at the
side of the house, everybody could hear the car on the gravel,
and then Mummy was blindfolded. We led her round the
side of the house, through the outside cloakrooms, round

the corner on the cobbles and then the blindfold was taken off and we all sang 'Happy Birthday' and everybody burst into tears. We'd made two thrones (very Polish) for my parents, which were standing in front of the swimming pool, and crowns for them to wear. And the children presented her with great bouquets of flowers and curtsied and kissed her hand.

My daughter and Gaba's two children, Isabella and Marc, did their party pieces. Lara played the recorder, Marc recited a little poem in Polish and Isabella, who was about three or four at the time, sang, 'Oh Mr Sun Sun, Mr Golden Sun, please shine down on me ... won't you shine down on me, please shine down on Bubby...'

Naturally, this made everybody cry all over again. Mama was already fairly ill with emphysema and, if she got overexcited or too exhilarated, she could sometimes get very breathless and uncomfortable, but she managed it extraordinarily well.

My father went to play tennis with Gaba. He'd lost rather a lot of weight and he was trying to play tennis and hold up his boxer shorts or his swimming trunks all the time and at one point he didn't manage to hold on and hit the ball at the same time – much to the delight and consternation of his grandchildren. It all ended with people being thrown into the swimming pool, everybody from the tiniest to the uncles and aunts up to the older brigade.

There was a fantastic array of food. It was a wonderful day and the actual show culminated with another song, written by my brother – 'Shine on Mama', which we three sisters sang and had recorded as an album to give her on the day. We still sing it on the anniversary of her death or on the anniversary of her birthday, and the children all either text or email or phone each other saying, 'Shine on Mama.' And she asked for a simple white cross to be put on her grave when she died, with 'Shine On Mama' on it.

In the first few months after Dennis left I had really hit rock bottom. I had such a hard time just gathering my strength again but slowly I started to make my way back. As it happens, a bit of work came along, a bit of money came along, a bit of support, the sun started to shine and I suddenly began to realise that I couldn't completely fall apart, not only because I had my daughter to look after but because I had myself to look after. The counselling started to help, I had a couple of good jobs and I began to see some sort of light at the end of the tunnel. I started to realise that actually this was not going to kill me.

Although I thought about Dennis a lot and still wondered about how he was and what was happening to him, and of course I still loved him and missed him, I didn't have a great deal of news, just the occasional bit in the papers would filter through from over there about him and his new lady friend. And, of course, I had my problems with the press here. They wanted to know in as much length and depth as possible what was happening with the money we owed on the movie. And when was Dennis coming back? Was he coming back? And did I know he had another woman over there?

I was playing Desiree in Stephen Sondheim's musical *A Little Night Music* down in Plymouth when, in the middle of the night, I got a phone call from the very drunk Mr Waterman, saying, 'I've made a terrible mistake, I want to come home.' My big song in the show was 'Send in the Clowns': 'Isn't it rich? / Are we a pair? / Me here at last on the ground / You in mid-air.' It seemed hideously apt.

Of course, the first thing that went through my mind was, 'Oh, she's left him.' Dennis was not a man who could spend any length of time on his own. I don't think he's ever spent any time alone. There were several very late-night conversations. Part of me, as the dumped woman, was desperately trying to believe he honestly did think he had made a mistake and that we were going to do everything possible to get back together again and make it work. But there was a niggling little voice that kept saying, 'You're going to have to really prove yourself, mate, before I can trust you again.' It was the small voice of reason, but once again I wasn't listening.

As Desiree in A Little Night Music,
singing 'Send in the Clowns'.

CHAPTER 13

OUT OF THE FRYING PAN INTO THE SERPENTINE INDEED!

When he came back I tried to persuade Dennis to go to counselling with me. My counsellor said, 'If you want to come and work on saving the relationship, then you've both got to face this together. There's no point just you having counselling, it's something you both need to do, either with the same counsellor or Dennis has to find somebody, and he also has to admit that drinking a lot changes his character and realise that if he wants to tackle the alcoholic side of things, he has to admit that he has a problem.'

And he did agree to go but it didn't last long.

He began to blame me for pulling him away from where he wanted to be, what he wanted to be doing and how he chose to spend his time. On the contrary, I tried to join him. When golf became the thing I took lessons and used to go and play with him. I played for about six months, and nine holes on a beautiful golf course on a sunny day was delicious but when we were playing with orange balls in the snow it became a pleasure I didn't share. I never got very good at it and I certainly didn't get obsessed with it but it started to become the most important thing in his life. He was a man who used to read quite a lot but suddenly the only magazines in the house were golf magazines. This was a man who once said to me, 'If I ever get hooked on that old man's game, kick me.' I appreciate one must allow men space for their hobbies, but it became an obsession. He would play almost every day if he wasn't working. And it wasn't just the whole day but drinking afterwards. And so it went on.

I became more and more suspicious and resentful about those long, heavily drink-fuelled sessions with his mates. When we first knew each other I made an effort to be there and he wanted me there with him. Now going off and getting drunk with the lads was an escape from the difficult atmosphere at home. He had known some of them for a very long time And because, to my mind, he only behaved badly after he'd been with them I suppose I would have preferred it if he didn't see them on a regular basis, although some of them I liked very much. I also knew that when they got together and had a long session there was a sort of character change, particularly vis-à-vis women.

There were times when he was still driving himself, and that was frightening. I would hear his car coming onto the drive and careering all over the place, then the car door opening and an unconscious man falling out, literally falling out. That he never actually injured or killed himself or anybody else during all those years when he was driving falling-down-drunk is astounding.

As far as getting stopped by the police was concerned, being Dennis Waterman could be either a blessing or a curse. Because of *Minder* and *The Sweeney* he'd had close contact with the force and I'm sure they enjoyed the programmes, so he was let off several times even though he had almost certainly had too much to drink. But sometimes it clearly went the other way.

On one occasion I was hauled up merely for being with him in a car. We were coming back from the West End after seeing a show and going out to dinner. It was the small hours of the morning and I was driving his big black BMW. I was stone-cold sober and he was very drunk next to me. Just as we were coming on to the M40 we were stopped by a police car. The young policeman's eyes were a picture. He asked the normal formal questions, to which I answered that I had not had a drink, which was completely true, then Dennis added, 'I fuckin' have ... plenty.' The policeman asked me to blow into the breathalyser, which I did with no visible results. He accused me of not blowing properly. Dennis's reply to that was unprintable and I was finally arrested for improper blowing and kept in the police station for about three hours until the desk sergeant arrived, checked and agreed I was completely sober.

Dennis lost his licence when he was caught on the M25 'veering from the hard shoulder to the nearside lane on a number of occasions,' as the police put it in court. He was nearly four times over the limit. He was banned from driving for three years, and because I then mostly drove him back and forth when he didn't have a chauffeur or a driver on hand, in a way I felt as though I was slightly more in control.

Then came the day when he got his licence back, the very day. We went out for a meal in Beaconsfield to celebrate, shared a bottle of wine, and the police were waiting and did him again for another three years. That was unnecessarily cruel. If he weren't Dennis Waterman it probably wouldn't have happened.

When there had been a horrible blow-up we had three or four days of supposedly coming back to some sort of under-standing. His way usually involved apologies and spending a lot of money on fantastic gifts. He would cry and I would cry and he would compose beautiful songs on the guitar and write me poetry and repeatedly say, 'I can't believe where I've taken you to and I can't believe how I've let you down and I can't tell you how ashamed I am and how much I love you,' and all the rest of it.

That was the recurring pattern. Things seemed to have a chance of being all right, then inevitably those good times would be ended by a particularly bad bender. One of his tricks when he was very drunk would be to turn the music in the house right up, off the scale, so the whole place was shaking, and if I was trying to get the children to sleep it became impossible. More often than not it was Bob Dylan, one of his great favourites. One of our love songs was 'Lay Lady Lay' (and we did have the big brass bed). And so he used to put Dylan on because he knew that would make me angry. I would go and turn the music down and he would come and turn it back up again and he would say, 'It's my fucking house and I'll have the fucking music up as loud as I fucking want.'

This all started escalating and getting nastier at the same time as my mother's health was failing, and indeed my father's – 1995. Plus, I'd gone to Tibet with a great friend of mine who was a Buddhist. Dennis was not religious and he was not very supportive about what he called my 'faddish behaviour'. There is an element of truth in that: I suppose I was and still am faddish about certain things, whether it's exercise or beliefs or looking into alternative cures such as massage and acupuncture. I get fixated for short amounts of time and tend to pour all my energies into them. Some are more short-lived than others but Buddhism was very powerful in my life and still is.

I was brought up Roman Catholic, of course, but there were lots of areas in the Catholic church that were difficult to come to terms with, things that I found really difficult to understand. I was, and had been for a quite a long time, on a quest for other spiritual meanings. I became involved with Nichiren Daishonin, which is a Japanese level of Buddhism.

And then my friend Nicole in the south of France asked me to accompany her on a trip to Kathmandu, and then from Kathmandu into Tibet.

It wasn't very usual then for tourists to go and it wasn't that easy to get into and you had to be very careful within Tibet. And travelling with us was a very high-up Buddhist guru who gave us instruction en route, as well as taking us to all the most famous monasteries. It was an extraordinary adventure but by no means a luxurious one. When I got back to England, Dennis's favourite line of attack was not to blame just me and my Polishness and my family, but also bloody Buddhism.

On my wonderful trip to Tibet, which I describe in the next chapter, I had met a very clever and high-powered and magnetic guru called Lama Norbu Repa. He came to stay a couple of times at Sheepcote when he was over here giving his teachings. And as it turned out, although Dennis battled against having anything to do with him, he was quite taken with him because besides being a Buddhist monk he was also a brilliant guitar player and he liked to have a drink and he was great company. Although Dennis steered clear of the lessons I was having, he actually had quite a good time with him and they sat jamming on guitars over a couple of glasses of red wine on more than one occasion.

By now my father had the beginnings of Alzheimer's and he was due to stay with me because his lady friend was away. I was alone in the house in Sheepcote. I'm not sure where

Dennis was, I think away working somewhere. My father had a habit of getting up in the middle of the night and looking for his German passport, thinking that the Germans might arrive at any moment. He was a very big man and because he had to sleep on a single, quite high bed, the only bedroom that was suitable for him was the kids' bedroom, when they weren't there. It happened to be right at the top of the stairs. I was terrified that when he got up, looking for whatever he used to look for in the middle of the night, he was going to fall down the stairs. And one night I woke up and he hadn't fallen down the stairs but he'd fallen out of bed and I couldn't lift him.

I had to call a private ambulance out, just to get him back into bed. I still had him for a few more days and I realised I just wasn't going to be able to cope with him. There was a little private nursing home in Beaconsfield run by Irish nuns and I went to see them and said, 'I'm having a very hard time at home with Daddy, he's not really a hundred per cent with us mentally and I'm extremely nervous about being on my own with him at home.' And they said he could go and stay there for two or three days.

My father was perfectly happy about that – he was very religious himself and very Catholic. He had been in the nursing home for about two days when Lama Norbu, the guru, arrived in England and I went to pick him up at the airport. He travelled in mufti, dressed in sort of ordinary although rather expensive clothes, not in the robes that he wore when he was at home. As soon as we got to our house he changed into his long carmine-coloured wrap-over skirt, his Tibetan jacket with bare arms and his earrings and his jewellery – quite exotic looking. And he had long, very dark hair, which he occasionally wore loose, but more often in a knot on the top of his head. And he had these extraordinarily piercing, very hypnotic dark blue eyes.

He said 'I suggest we go and see your father.' I hadn't told him anything about my father either having been there or not being there any more. I said, 'Lama, I don't think it's a very good idea. My father's deeply Roman Catholic. He doesn't really know anything about my Buddhism and he's not very well.' And Lama Norbu said, 'Trust me, we'll go to see your father.' And there was no way you argued with Lama Norbu. So we had something to eat, got in the car and went to the nursing home.

A tiny Irish nun called Sister Bernadette opened the door and there was the lama, in his robes with his long hair loose. She did a double take and he put his hand on top of her head and gave her a blessing. Then we went to go up the stairs and I knew my father's room was at the top, so I said to Lama Norbu, 'Wait here a minute.' The sister knocked on the door and I opened it. My father was lying on a single hospital bed about a foot-and-a-half too small for him, reading the Polish newspaper upside down. And I stood in the doorway and said, 'Papi, I brought somebody special to see you.' And there is

Lama Norbu, backlit in the entrance to my father's room, and my father looked up and said, 'Rasputin!' in an awed whisper. He was absolutely convinced, and he did look a bit like Rasputin, I have to say.

Lama Norbu played the game, sat on the bed, took my father's hands in his and acted as if he was whoever my father wanted him to be. Extraordinary.

The mystical Lama Norbu Repa.

CHAPTER 14

PASSING THE BLESSING ON

Tibet was a place I had dreamed of visiting ever since reading a book called *The Third Eye* by Lobsang Rampa at the age of about fifteen. Buddhism, with its belief in one's own higher power, had always attracted me. I had had the great privilege of meeting His Holiness the Dalai Lama on a couple of occasions and the knowledge that I was going to visit the home from where he'd been exiled, and the seat of Buddhism, was immensely exciting. In 1995, when my mother's health was failing and things were going very wrong at home, Nicole Chaniac, a great friend of mine and a devoted practising Buddhist, invited me to go with a small group of friends. We were to meet in Kathmandu, one of my favourite places in the world. I had already been there twice, once on my second Blashford-Snell expedition and once to do a small travelogue for the BBC.

Leaving England on a grey, drizzly, autumn day with what felt like the beginnings of a head cold, I flew Royal Nepalese

Airlines, stopping off briefly in Frankfurt and Dubai. On the last leg of the journey I was seated next to a fascinating Indian gentleman, an architect working in Riyadh, who was travelling back to Delhi for a puja – a period of fasting and prayer with his family. We talked about Hinduism and Buddhism. For the last twenty minutes of the flight we had the most spectacular views of the Annapurna range, with amazing cloud formations that looked like pale pink ice.

The monsoons had just finished in Kathmandu and it was warm and dry. We rode in a very rickety old taxi to the Yak & Yeti Hotel, avoiding sacred cows and schoolchildren, to meet Nicole. We had a quick meal and hit the sack to prepare for a seven o'clock start for the first of our long drives to the Nepalese border.

It was an eight-hour drive in two four-wheel-drive trucks. Beyond the filthy suburbs of the town the scenery becomes beautiful: steep green hillsides interspersed with tumbling waterfalls and small villages. At the border there was about an hour of paperwork then we were put on the back of a cattle truck to rattle up a hill on a narrow road with the most terrifying drops on either side. Every so often a huge herd of sheep or goats stopped our progress but it didn't matter – time has no meaning here.

On the Chinese–Tibetan side of the border we were immediately surrounded by Tibetans asking for photographs of the Dalai Lama. We had been forbidden to bring any with us.

The atmosphere was claustrophobic and very smelly and we made our way to the border hotel, where we enjoyed a small picnic before going walkabout. The streets were crowded and everywhere we went we were followed by a large crowd of locals, all fascinated by my camera and wanting to have their pictures taken – loads of colourful children, beautiful women in full traditional dress and Sherpa carrying huge loads.

Back at the hotel we took our first dose of something that is supposed to help with altitude sickness. It had pretty immediate strange side effects: tingling in the arms and legs and a constant desire to pee. The floor in our bedroom was filthy. And there was no running water, but the sheets looked more or less OK. So, an early night.

We had thirteen hours of driving ahead of us, and the roads were very changeable, sometimes quite decent and tarmacked then suddenly long stretches of packed mud and huge potholes, and the suspension in those trucks was non-existent. By midday we were at 3,500 metres. Breathing began to be a problem. Every time we stopped we were surrounded by begging children, but we had been warned to keep our presents for the monasteries or schools so they would be fairly shared. The kiddies all had frostbitten cheeks and runny noses and hacking coughs and very chapped hands.

The traditional Tibetan house is square and one storey with chortens at the four corners – these are little piles of stones of varying heights which hold prayer flags. The houses are divided into compartments, and are shared by yaks and dogs and donkeys as well as human beings, each benefiting from the other for warmth and comfort. Everywhere is pervaded by a very distinctive smell which comes from the traditional Tibetan tea, made with rancid butter.

As we climbed the air got thinner and thinner. The road got rougher and bumpier and the scenery got more and more bleak. It is supposed to be the roughest terrain in the world and because of the height any slight exertion resulted in dizziness and a feeling of weakness and vulnerability – not pleasant.

We stopped at a place called Old Tingri for our first taste of traditional Tibetan food in a local farmstead: yak tea, dumplings with some dubious filling, and rice. Big mistake! Walking around this little nomadic settlement Nicole and I watched an extraordinary scene: a man had a sheep in his lap while his wife was softly stroking the sheep's head and singing to it. Very gently the man took a knife and inserted it into the sheep's chest, put his hand in and took out the heart, chanting all the while. The sheep made not a sound, just quietly expired as the woman carried on singing to it.

Soon after the meal we were stricken with serious stomach cramps, and car stops became more and more frequent. By this time there was hardly any cover at all, so we just did the best we could. We were all feeling sick and weak now and all of us, apart from our two guides, were suffering. At 4,300 metres we caught our first sight of Everest – not a cloud in sight, this huge iced meringue standing out against a vast empty plateau, dazzlingly white against a blue sky.

We stayed overnight in a place called Shigatse, Tibet's second largest city. I felt as if I had been on a ship for a week – wobbly, seasick and with a pounding head. The beds were rock-hard and the water, what there was of it, dark brown. But we did manage to get some sleep.

The following day we visited Tashilhunpo monastery. Huge. And the monks were certainly wise to the benefits of demanding money for photographs. Hundreds of altars, some ornate and smothered in gold and others dusty and faded and unkempt. Monks of varying sizes and ages kept up a constant chant while filling the candle bowls with yak butter, which gave off an insistent, very pungent and nauseating smell. Hundreds of statues of gods and bodhisattvas, prayer wheels and bells. Within the prayer wheels and the big drums outside the monasteries were the words: 'om mani padme hum', prayers for the salvation of mankind, and everyone who passes the drums turns them in a clockwise direction, the theory being that these prayers are constantly being released into the atmosphere. There were hundreds of groups of Tibetan pilgrims, some of them very ornately dressed and coiffed, placing offerings of food and money and flowers on the altars of the various deities, and some of them prostrate. They had travelled long distances to get to this sacred place and many of them were really very old. It was a touching sight.

The monks seemed to have a wonderful sense of humour, constantly giggling like children. There was a warmth and a feeling of community and serenity in all the monasteries, a feeling of safety and happiness. Onwards to Gyantse: suddenly the countryside began to look more prosperous, with cultivated fields with proper irrigation channels, avenues of trees which to me looked like eucalyptus, yaks and horses threshing grain as the peasants chanted rhythmically. Everyone was very friendly and welcoming. It was almost impossible to take candid photographs: the minute they saw the camera they all lined up making silly faces.

The following morning, after an almost-decent night's sleep, we set off again. In terms of altitude this would be the highest day. Now we were all feeling it. The persistent dust everywhere was probably partly to blame for stuffed-up noses and sore throats. We climbed and climbed and arrived finally at Yamdrok Tso, one of Tibet's most sacred lakes, at over 5,000 metres. The colours ranged from the palest of translucent turquoise to the deepest cobalt. Huge and peaceful and so beautiful. We found a secluded spot and suddenly out of nowhere we were invaded by hordes of curious children who wanted to share our picnic – for most of them probably their first proper meal for a while. Obviously we had no common language, but we were all soon giggling with them and there was a delightful feeling of sharing and togetherness.

Next stop, Lhasa. The roads were precipitous and there

were signs of many landslides, but soon there were proper tarmac roads, cars and motorbikes and many Chinese army trucks, and the people were dressed in a mix of traditional and Western clothes. We passed an enormous painting on the rocks of Shakyamuni, the Buddha of compassion. Legend has it that this painting spontaneously appeared. We caught a brief glimpse of the Potala Palace, once the home of the exiled Dalai Lama.

The main entrance to Lhasa was closed and we were diverted via a huge cement factory belching forth smoke and dust. Every blade of grass, every car and every human being looked grey. We were directed into a field and were surprised to hear that each car arriving at the Holiday Inn had to be washed and sparkling. Never mind that we sitting inside were filthy and dusty – Chinese demands. Their presence was now very visible and somewhat forbidding.

By now we were all hugely looking forward to a bath and a decent bed and a hairwash. It was like Holiday Inn hotels all over the world: comfortable and bland, but with running hot water and even a TV. And I managed to get a connection to ring home and speak to Dennis and Lara.

Dinner. Looking and feeling almost human. And then Nicole and I went to meet her lama, Norbu Repa, who, as I have said, later met my father – who mistook him for Rasputin – and even managed to charm Dennis, who was not well disposed towards Buddhism, especially mine. Lama

Norbu is in fact Belgian, a high master and teacher and a yogi. Slight, with the most piercing blue eyes, thick beard and long black hair, he was traditionally dressed in long crimson robes. He spoke excellent English, French and Tibetan and he had a very arresting and imposing personality.

Since we had run out of the altitude medication the lama arranged an appointment for me with a Tibetan doctor who had supposedly looked after the Dalai Lama. A dreadful sleepless night, and the following morning at breakfast the chefs and waitresses looked so grubby that any little appetite left us entirely. Lama Norbu was now dressed in a long white skirt, a saffron top and a burgundy shawl. His hair was in a topknot and he wore heavy ivory bangles and shell hoops in his ears, very imposing and theatrical. We set off to visit Tashi Kang, a monastery he was rebuilding.

All the workers we met and all the women and children bowed their heads for his blessing. It was a gloriously bright and sunny day and we were taken for a tour by the lama. The monks sat on the steps studying their scriptures, the workmen were chanting and smiling as they worked on their given tasks, some of them painting intricate designs on the doors and walls. And I was allowed to photograph and video to my heart's content. Up on the roof of the lama's private apartment we had several hours of teachings about the Buddhist religion. It was appealing and emotional and fascinating and it demanded an enormous amount of discipline but Lama

Norbu had a hypnotic quality and huge charisma. I could quite see why Nicole was so taken by him.

On the way back to Lhasa I discussed with him the possibility of one of the charities I am involved with, Children in Crisis, becoming engaged with exiled and orphaned Tibetan children. Back to the hotel and after a quick wash and brush-up Nicole and I went to the Jokhang temple and the Barkhor, the central marketplace. It was heaving with pilgrims and tourists and monks, traditionally dressed Tibetan nomads, both men and women, with huge lumps of turquoise and amber threaded through their finely braided hair, and silk turbans decorated with silver and precious stones.

Some of the men were wearing sheepskin-lined brocade coats decorated round the edges with leopard skin. The ladies carried their babies in the papoose style. There were bells and sirens, loud Chinese music, shouting, chanting, laughter and bartering and of course all the pilgrims carried their prayer wheels. There were people eating, sleeping, chatting, arguing and prostrating themselves. A riot of colour and movement, sound and smell, all pervaded by a strong sense of spirituality. But there was a huge discordant note – the Chinese militia were out in force and making their presence felt.

There were hundreds of stalls selling colourful rugs, great strings of precious stones, wall hangings, thangkas, musical instruments, traditional woven Tibetan boots, rucksacks and jewellery. We bartered for a few souvenirs but after a couple of hours we were both struggling with our breathing and we went back to the hotel for a little rest prior to that evening's meeting with the Tibetan doctor.

He was elderly and rotund with a warm kind face and incredibly hot hands. He sat cross-legged and, through an interpreter, asked to see my tongue, looked at my eyes and my fingernails and asked whether I had heart problems, back pain or arthritis. I answered appropriately and he said he could feel that I was carrying a lot of anxiety that compounds altitude sickness. He told me that my greatest worries would resolve themselves but it would be a long and hard battle. I knew what he was talking about! He then gave me a tiny pill wrapped in red silk and tied with a silver thread, instructed me to crush and steep it in boiling water that night and drink it down the following morning at dawn. He blessed me and I left feeling very calm. I followed his instructions. The pill was very highly perfumed when crushed. I managed to sleep slightly better and drink the potion as commanded at dawn. Magically, or thanks to autosuggestion, it did help.

Thank goodness, because we were off to Tsurphu monastery, which is another 1,000 metres higher, one of the most famous monasteries in Tibet and the seat of the boy, then ten years old, who had been found age seven and recognised in the traditional manner as the seventeenth Karmapa Lama.

After a light breakfast we loaded our gear on to the trucks and set off – 70 kilometres, about three hours. The air got thinner as we entered the most beautiful valley. Steep craggy ravines covered with sparse vegetation of varying shades of gold and brown. Yaks grazed peacefully and babbling brooks trickled down to left and right. We saw nomadic tents as well as mounted Tibetan nomads on heavily decorated ponies. Sheep, goats and yaks with tinkling bells took no heed of the cars and moved out of the way only if and when they felt like it. Lama Norbu informed us we would be meeting the Rinpoche, the abbot of a monastery which had been totally destroyed by the Chinese and was in the process of being rebuilt. It used to house over 600 monks. Now there were only eighty. All the buildings as we drove into the courtyard were in a serious state of disrepair and neglect but there was an air of peace and tranquillity as in all of these holy places. We were ushered into a small room where the Rinpoche sat, prayer beads in hand, and we all knelt in front of him and handed him the traditional khata, a thin silk scarf which he blessed and put round our necks. He then tied thin red silk thread round our necks – a special blessing which you are supposed to keep on for three days then pass on to another person or animal. It was only after two hours in the presence of this holy man that we learnt he was totally blind. We had a guided tour of the monastery and a detailed account of the dreadful invasion by the Chinese and the torture and terror inflicted on the monks.

The following day we were due to visit the Potala Palace and the university of Tibetan medicine, which promised to be another extraordinary and thought-provoking day. The combination of excitement and breathing difficulties made sleep hard to come by. The next morning we drove to the Potala Palace, now no longer a working monastery but a place of pilgrimage and a museum with more than a thousand rooms. We were dismayed to find over 1,000 pilgrims waiting to go in. After several hours of queuing it was apparent we would not make it, so we decided to walk around, photograph what we could and just drink in the atmosphere. There were hundreds of beggars, some of them very badly disfigured, some missing limbs and others obviously suffering from leprosy. The lama advised us not to give them money but to sit and talk and spend time with them, since in the Tibetan religion disfigurements and suffering are deemed to be in atonement for wrong deeds performed in a previous life or lives.

On our last night we joined the lama and a very high-up rinpoche and his wife for our farewell meal, eaten cross-legged with traditional Tibetan music. And a wonderful meal it was. Though the plane was not until 10 a.m. we had to wake up at 5 a.m. to get to the airport.

The air was cold as the dawn broke. We were all quiet and in awe of these last few days. The airport was total chaos. Monks and locals and tourists, four hours of queuing, but we all felt an internal peace. It had been an extraordinary journey, physically hard but mentally so stimulating and thought-provoking.

On the plane – Chinese, so the legroom was laughable –

I was sandwiched between Tibetan pilgrims. The smell was simply overpowering but the views of the Himalayas were breathtaking. Again, Everest: goodbye, magical mystical country, never to be forgotten. Now back to the traumas of Sheepcote!

CHAPTER 15

'WHY CAN'T YOU JUST IGNORE ME?'

The physical part of my relationship with Dennis had always been incredibly important but it started to be used as a weapon – the best part of breaking up is making up and all that. There would be a lot of loving and affection, which I think he and I both needed. But when somebody's ugly on drink, they become clumsy and pawing and you can tell there's no real feeling in it.

I knew the pattern would repeat itself and there would only be a certain amount of time before he would go on the next bender with his mates and come back aggressive towards me and angry with me, absolutely not behaving like the man I had fallen in love with. And then there would be flowers and writings and songs – he wrote a beautiful song for me called 'Indian Silk'. And for four or five days everything would be wonderful and peaceful and for a foolishly long time I would persuade myself to think, 'This is it. Everything's going to be fine.' And he would stop drinking for a bit and proudly say, 'See, I have no problems with alcohol. I can give it up when I want to.'

When he was drunk he cried very easily and copiously which reinforced my belief that the drink was used to help him do or say what he was incapable of doing or saying unless he was drunk. There was a pattern of going out with the lads and staying out until the wee hours of the morning, having promised to get back for dinner. One or two hours late is one thing but saying you'd be back at nine o'clock in the evening and rolling up at three o'clock in the morning absolutely unrecognisable is something else. Not only did it make me angry, it terrified me, especially if he was driving. I was frightened on his account and on my own.

I never had the stalwartness or the bravery or the self-control or the common sense to ignore what was coming home. As I've said, I could tell when it was bad from the way his key turned in the lock and from the behaviour of the dog or cats. Obviously it was more disturbing if my child or his children were in the house as well, and I would aggravate the situation by trying to get an explanation from somebody who could hardly put two words together. That infuriated him. I think he blamed me for pulling him away from where he wanted to be, surrounded by his drinking mates who were never going to ask difficult questions and who didn't make him feel more guilty or unhappy than he already was.

He knew he was coming back to an angry or tearful or frightened or frustrated or furious spouse. Of course I can understand that was difficult for him. And when he was sober he said to me, 'Why can't you just leave well alone? If I come back in that state why can't you just ignore me? Go to the other end of the house, whatever, and don't stick the needle in. Don't press my button.'

I found that very difficult to do, though I did do it a few times. On one particular occasion it had very nasty repercussions: I went up to bed and took myself into the spare room and he came in and knocked the door down and was physically unpleasant and dragged me back to our room. I always knew it was the drink that made him behave like this. It was by no means a regular occurrence but there were one or two moments when I was really scared of him and he either didn't realise what he was doing or the following day didn't remember what he had done. Sometimes he was gripped by completely unjustified jealousy of one kind or another and I also sensed a dangerous sort of fear in him: fear that he had gone too far so might as well go further.

Sometimes he was so drunk that maybe the things he was threatening to do, or looked as if he was threatening to do, would never have happened because he wouldn't have been able to keep his balance for long enough. But there were a couple of times when I had to call the police out.

I certainly did not tell my mother or my father, because I

didn't want to worry them. They knew we had serious troubles because they had lived through the whole business of him going off with Fiona. He did once try to lift his hand to my mother – only once – and not in a truly threatening way. He was a bit drunk and he just raised his arm above her and she said, 'Don't you try it on with me.' I think maybe my youngest sister knew and certainly my friend Michèle Clarke, who was at that time someone I saw on virtually a daily basis.

Perhaps I should have played him at his own game and changed the locks and not allowed him back into the house. Certainly nothing justified the things he did. I thought about leaving many times, and then somehow he would always make me believe I should stay. When things got really bad, he would realise it and show remorse and tenderness and pull me back into the feeling that this time it was really going to be different and it wouldn't happen again. This went on for many months. Three particularly horrid days suddenly morphed into apologies, beautiful letters and songs and assurances of love and 'you must help me' and 'yes, we'll go to counselling and we'll get it all cleared up and everything will be fine'. And I believed it!

Of course I was worried about losing him. This was the man I had broken my first marriage for and antagonised and hurt a lot of people for, and although I always knew that in some respects we were chalk and cheese, this was the man I fell deeply in love with and there was a large part of me that never fell out of love because I don't believe that happens. There was also the sadness of losing what I'd fought so hard for. A lot of people thought it was crazy of me to expect it to last. I had a couple of girlfriends who were absolutely adamant that it was obvious nothing was going to change. I remember my counsellor saying at one point, 'Shit or get off the pot. You either change your attitude, adjust to the situation, start to behave differently, stop arguing with him. Or you must leave.'

The realistic thing would have been to recognise that this was the man he was. It's not as if the drink was anything new, it was there from the very beginning. It's just that he made an enormous effort at the beginning and less and less effort as time went on. Then there were the betrayals and the desertion. Of course I didn't want another divorce. Of course I didn't want to leave our beautiful house in the country. Of course, right until the very end, until the few bouts of physical danger, I believed that something was going to miraculously turn things around. Because, despite everything, the feelings that brought us together still survived. It was always a hugely charged relationship, physically and emotionally.

❦

Our beloved dog Silky developed cancer of the bones and we took her through all the traditional radiology and the rest of it, and then I went to see an alternative practitioner who suggested crystals and things like that, which in the beginning

Dennis found weird, but anything to extend the life of this dog who was so loved by both of us. And we did prolong it for about another year with alternative therapies and then I remember coming down one morning and she was sitting in the kitchen with this hugely swollen paw. We couldn't get her into the car any more to take her to the vet and the vet had to come over and put her down in our arms. And I've never seen anybody cry like that – like Dennis did. He was a very strange mixture of emotions and doubts.

He was aware of his own talent and definitely aware of his own magnetism. But whether he actually had a sense of wrongdoing when he had his affairs or got ugly mentally and physically I'm not quite sure. I think he might have thought that this was his prerogative as a man.

In the early days, when I used to sit and watch him quietly get drunk when we were at home together – and before I started drinking at all – he was rather funny and warm, occasionally maudlin, and sometimes there was that sort of drunken fumbling that I didn't like, but mostly there was nothing ugly or unpleasant.

When the house was full of the blokes getting gently pissed, with the women sometimes joining them, it was fine. Later, it seemed to me, he would come back from benders with his mates in attacking mode because he felt I had forced him to come back. And I got the impression that he had been allowed his drinking time in his previous marriage.

Undoubtedly there are things you forgive at the start of relationships, partly because you believe the reason they are the way they are is a hangover from before and you're going to make it better. In the early days he made a serious effort to keep the promise to be back in the evening and be part of the family. He wanted me with him all the time at the beginning.

It's really hard looking back now. I sometimes think to myself, if I had been one of those women capable of weathering the infidelities, if I hadn't taken it so painfully personally, if I hadn't taken it as a direct insult and a direct hurt and as a few steps down the road to destruction, if I had been able to ignore it and take it more in my stride, I wonder whether we would have survived; if I had accepted he would have the odd dalliance and that every so often he would need to go off and get pissed and this was just how our life was going to be.

But I wasn't like that. I wanted to change it. I wanted it to go back to what it had been before and I wanted his reassurance when he had been unfaithful that this was never going to happen again. For me, fidelity was very important, for him much less so.

What a surprise! With Michael Aspel at the Harlequin Theatre in Redhill, Surrey, 1995. (© Andy Huntley)

CHAPTER 16

THAT WAS MY LIFE

'**G**o and get some sleep, my darlings, it will not be tonight.' These were the last words I heard my mama speak. It's a hard picture to go back to but nevertheless a beautiful and privileged one. It was close to Christmas 1995, just a day after I had been surprised, as most 'victims' are, by *This Is Your Life*.

I was playing the Wicked Queen to Trevor Bannister's dame in *Snow White* at the Harlequin Theatre at Redhill in Surrey. We were taking the curtain call for the second show of the day when I noticed rather a lot of commotion in the auditorium. People were standing and clapping and what looked like television cameras were moving towards us. A bit perplexed and rather longing to get out of my heavy costume and drive home, I smiled and moved backwards away from the cameras that were now coming up on to the stage.

Then I realised what was going on – they had come to get Trevor, a brilliant comic actor and famous pantomime dame, for *This Is Your Life*. He would be wafted from the stage to a studio to have his whole life laid out before an audience of millions with the help of his friends, relatives and possibly famous adversaries from down the years, there to praise him as well as doubtless provide a few embarrassing moments, with the whole story set down in the big red book held at that time by Michael Aspel. Trevor was to be the latest in a line of 'victims' that stretched back decades.

I looked at him and winked and, stepping back, trod on someone's toe. I turned round to say sorry and saw it was Mr Aspel's foot. Suddenly the rest of the cast were no longer so closely grouped round me and Michael was handing *me* the famous red book. The first notes of the intro music filled the theatre. I was totally shocked and unprepared and quite honestly not too happy about it because my life was not in a good way at the time, to put it mildly. But I tried to be gracious and, I suppose, grateful.

Having been a guest on other people's *Life* and knowing how it worked, I wondered how on earth it could have been kept a secret from me while they were getting it together, especially by my daughter, who was about fifteen at the time and had driven in to the theatre with me every day during the school holidays to look after the pantomime babes. She must have known about this for at least a month. As both my parents were already very unwell I could imagine how difficult the secrecy and preparation must have been for my family. My immediate thoughts were for their welfare in particular.

As soon as Michael Aspel had finished on stage I was hustled off to my dressing room with a minder, who from then on never left my side. Maybe they thought I was going to run away. Apparently it has happened before. Several times.

Because I had no idea this was going to happen I had come to the theatre in ordinary work clothes – jeans, a warm sweater, boots and so on. It certainly wasn't the sort of outfit I would want to appear on TV in. It was already well past 10.30 in the evening so there was no time to go home to get an outfit. I was told not to worry, Dennis had picked something out for me to wear and it was waiting in the Teddington recording studios.

The most important thing was to get cracking as soon as possible because my family and all the invited guests from near and far had been waiting and rehearsing all afternoon and of course everyone was tired. I was really worried about my parents though I was sure they would be in the best of hands, surrounded by my mother's siblings and her children.

The other huge worry, of course, was Dennis. Things had been going from bad to worse in their usual manner but we would have to put on a great united front of solidarity and togetherness. What's more, he had been at the studio all day with some of his mates. How much drinking had gone on?

We sped off to Teddington in a chauffeur-driven limo. I was not even allowed to share a car with my daughter; she had another one all to herself! Once we arrived I was whisked in great secrecy through to a dressing room, where I was given about an hour for hair and make-up. There were wonderful nibbles, and flowers and drink in abundance. Then I checked the outfit Dennis had picked for me to wear on national TV for this most special occasion.

It was a bottle-green lounging-around-the-house comfortable kaftan with baggy harem pants and flat sandals! Hardly the sexy, confident image I would have liked to portray. I am sure he didn't do it on purpose but I couldn't understand why he had chosen such an outfit from a wardrobe full of sophisticated, smart, elegant clothes much more fitting for such an occasion.

Anyway, no time to dwell on that, I was being hurried up. It was late, everyone was tired and we had a show to record. There would of course be at least a couple of people who had been flown in from the other side of the world. I knew these were the high points and I had a pretty good idea who those long-distance specials would be. And I was right – Veronica Hammond, one of my first and dearest friends from boarding school had come all the way from Kenya and, all the way from Colombia, Don MacIver from drama school. They were amongst the handful of people who have been close to me for decades.

As it turned out it was wonderful. My headmistress from boarding school, my hot-air-balloon pilot teacher and nearly all the family from near and far had come. My mother's two beloved brothers, Jas from Munich and Arthur from Dublin; my lovely sister Gaba from America; my wonderful youngest sister Anna and my gorgeous talented brother Andrew. Then there was Charlotte Cornwell, one of the three Little Ladies from *Rock Follies* days, Howard Schuman, the *Rock Follies* author, and Susie Penhaligon who had been at drama school with me; Anita Dobson, another drama school friend, and Christopher Timothy, with whom I did my first pantomime, which also starred Les Dawson and Bernard Bresslaw; and there were also good mutual friends of Dennis's and mine, including Warren and Michèle Clark, who remain close to me still, even though there was a bit of a hiccup when Dennis and I broke up.

There were representatives from some of the charities I had worked for – John Gray from the Red Cross, and Virginia McKenna's son Will Travers, who is now director of the Born Free Foundation; Colonel John Blashford-Snell, with whom I had done two extraordinary life-changing working expeditions in India and Nepal; my first agent; all the cast of the pantomime and of course my beloved parents and the children: my step-daughters Hannah and Julia from Dennis's previous marriage, and my own precious, beautiful daughter, Lara.

It was a moving and evocative hour. There was one glaring omission – Krysia Podleska, my oldest friend from pre-school Brownie days. I have known her virtually all my life and we got into all sorts of scrapes and adventures as naughty young girls. We started working together in the Polish theatre when we were in our early teens. Sadly I don't see her so often because she lives in Poland, but we are in regular contact.

Later I found out there had been something of a battle between my family and Dennis about the sort of people that were to be picked out of my address book and invited onto the programme, and I discovered how hard all this planning and secrecy had been for my mother, who was already ill and weak.

Mama knew very little about *This Is Your Life*. Quite rightly she saw the family and the dearest friends who had meant a great deal to me as the most important people to invite. But of course, since this was a TV programme Thames wanted a smattering of 'lardies' (celebs) and there was limited room for so many to make an appearance or to have a seat in the audience. This had resulted in several skirmishes between my youngest sister Anna, in charge of arranging the family side of things, and my husband.

Mama had got it into her head that *This Is Your Life* meant this is the end of your career, and because she knew how rocky Dennis and I were she thought Dennis had somehow engineered it.

Tellingly, when Michael Aspel asked her to address a few words to me she said: 'You have many challenges and loves in your life. I want to take this opportunity to congratulate you for the first part of your life and wish you strength for the second part of your life both in your personal life and on the stage.'

The programme went very well and then there was a marvellous hoolie laid on with loads of food and drink and an opportunity to chat to all the family and friends. By the end of the recording it was already well after midnight and Mama was feeling very weak. She was driven back almost immediately to her little flat. She was already on oxygen 24/7 and having great difficulty with her breathing, and you could see the programme had really drained her. I should have gone back with her but I couldn't.

This was a great honour for me and I had to stay and spend time with my guests. But she shouldn't have been allowed to go home on her own. That will always be on my conscience. My father at least had his girlfriend Tania to look after him but Mama was all alone in her flat.

It was a very late night and I had two shows the next day. Obviously all the pantomime cast had been invited to the recording and the party, so at the matinée the next day we were in a great mood but a bit weary. Straight after the second show I staggered home and to bed to be woken by a phone call from Hammersmith hospital at three in the morning. Mama had been taken in. They did not think she was going to last the night. I raced out of bed into my car and drove to London hoping and praying that I would still find her alive. I met my sisters and brother and a very pregnant sister-in-law around Mama's bed in a small, softly lit ward. She looked peaceful, though her breathing was laboured. We were all quiet and controlled and praying in our own ways and supporting each other as best we could.

The corridors were full of her brothers and sisters, and everyone was together as if somehow Mama had ordained this departure to coincide with *This is Your Life*, knowing she would have all her family round her. As Gaba, Anna, Andrew, Jacqui and my stepbrother's wife Winsome and I sat or knelt around Mama she suddenly softly uttered those words in her adorable Polish accent: 'Go and get some sleep, my darlings, it will not be tonight.' And we did, and it wasn't.

It was the next night, in an almost total repetition of the circumstances. Again, after two shows, a telephone call from the hospital and a mad rush in the early hours of the morning to be by Mama's bedside. She had already had the last sacraments from a priest and was lying very peacefully in her little cubicle. My brother and I were on either side of her head and my other two sisters were at her feet, all of us praying and watching Mama and relieved that she did not have pain. It was a very special time for us, coming together and sharing something we knew was a huge moment as well as a tragic one. I must have nodded off, as the next thing I remember was Gaba saying, 'She has gone.'

It was totally surreal, very peaceful, Mama's beautiful face looked twenty years younger, the stress lines from her breathing difficulties had disappeared. She looked serene and tranquil and at peace. We were dumbstruck. Time stood still. This was truly the end of an era, not just for her children together round her bed, but for the whole family. My mother was an incredible force, a true matriarch loved by everybody. She had had so much influence on everyone's life. She had not a single jot of bitterness in her body. Life had treated her pretty cruelly at times. Her experiences during the Second World War were torturous and her arrival here as a refugee extremely difficult. Then for years she was virtually a single mother while my father was forced to leave England for work in Germany. In her later life she suffered emotionally from being left by her beloved second husband. And yet she had found an inner peace with her God about everything.

She was an inspirational, caring and loving mother, sister, grandmother, wife, friend and daughter and a wonderful woman to everyone who knew her. She truly touched people's lives and still does.

Because my sister Gaba was a trained nurse, we were given the very special privilege of laying Mama out. We gently washed, creamed and powdered her poor, tired, ravaged body, combed her hair and put a rosary and a rose in her hands, and half crying, half smiling, with a great love and coming together for us her children, we felt the circle closing. How wonderful to have been given this opportunity to be at the end of our mama's life as she had been at the beginning of ours.

The producers of *This Is Your Life* sweetly put at the beginning of the programme that it was dedicated to her memory. To this day I have not been able to watch it. It was the last footage of both my beloved parents – three weeks later my father also left us.

Losing your parents is a real time of growing up, not just because you realise you are now top of the tree, so to speak, but because parents are irreplaceable. Their love is totally unconditional.

My father, though separated from my mother for over twenty-five years, had always remained the closest of friends with her. Even though he had had a lovely and very special lady friend, Tatiana Prigorowska, since the time he had worked and lived in Munich, he and my mother saw each other often and had the greatest love and respect for each other.

On all special occasions, even during the time my mother was married to her second husband, my father was always there. Indeed, while my mother and her second husband Nicky were still living in the family home in Willesden Green it was not unusual at Sunday lunch to have my father at one end of the table and my stepfather at the other end.

My father, who was ten years older than my mother, had been wrongly diagnosed with Parkinson's and there were signs of other underlying problems. For some time he had been showing signs of dementia. He was a very proud man and found the descent into loss of control horribly difficult to cope with, and my sisters and I will always be grateful to the wonderful love and dedication given to him by Tania right until the end. My father had taken the loss of my mother very badly.

It was almost as if the light went out behind his eyes when we told him. Shortly afterwards his condition worsened and he was taken to hospital.

Dennis, who had behaved with great respect throughout the period when we lost Mama, had gone off to South Africa to play golf. I was in rehearsals for a play called *Presents from the Past* in north London. Strangely, it was about a family coming together to go through their mother's house after her death.

I got a call from my sister Gaba saying that Papa was in a bad state. I rushed out of the rehearsal rooms desperately hoping to be there at the end. Sadly I missed his passing by about five minutes. Thank God Tania and Gaba were with him. It was almost too much to bear. We three sisters were in a real state of shock.

About a week later Dennis rang from South Africa. He asked me whether I had cheered up. I said not really because Papa had died. There was a long pause on the phone and then he said, 'Fuck, I suppose that means I have to come back!' That was more or less the last straw for me.

They wanted to do a post-mortem because there was a suspicion that Papa might have had cancer of the bones, but as a family we decided against it. What's the point of cutting him up at that age? We decided to take his ashes back to Poland.

We three sisters with our children and our stepmother arrived to an enormous fanfare, with church festivities, army, boy scouts and all the local people turning out. It was all beautifully arranged and incredibly moving. The people there had not really known my father personally – he'd met them once – but they knew about his career and the history of his family, which was so closely associated with the area.

A fine gravestone had been made and etched and a beautiful place in the cemetery had been specially prepared. There were speeches and meals and evenings spent singing and dancing, and the local band turned out. We felt delighted that Papa was given such an incredible send-off. It was extraordinary, really like something out of another century.

With Mama.

CHAPTER 17

MAMA'S LONGEST JOURNEY

My mother was enormously important in my life and even after all these years I feel her loss profoundly. She was always loving and generous. She was weakened by mental illness and during the war she endured hardships that seemed almost unbearable. Understandably, and to my great delight as a little girl, Mama would often hark back to pre-war Poland, her blissful childhood, her love for her parents and the wonderful things the family did at all the different times of the year at their beautiful house and estate in the country.

Only very rarely did she talk about the bad times. If we asked her a direct question and she'd had a couple of drinks, she might talk about the concentration camp – it was no secret and we knew it was clear in her memory but however hard we tried to draw her out on the minutiae of camp life, we were never very successful.

I think the closest that she got was when she talked about

these memories with an interviewer from the BBC. Probably she found it easy to tell it to a stranger. Here is some of what she told her about what happened after she and the family had fled from Poland with chauffeur, nanny and maid, and a convoy of at least twelve other cars. She was eighteen years old and the eldest daughter.

After a torturous journey through Romania they arrived very tired and hungry in Belgrade. They met White Russians who had been there since 1917 but were still dreaming of returning to Tsarist Russia. My mother recalled:

At the time I thought, 'How can they be thinking about such things more than twenty years on?' Later, when I was in England many years after the Second World War, I finally understood what these Russians were dreaming about.

She goes on:

We stayed in Belgrade from the autumn of 1939 until 1941. The Serbs were incredibly kind, helping us when they could, providing clothes and feeding us in very cheap Russian restaurants. We sold our cars and my mother sold her jewellery and somehow we had enough to survive. At some point we thought about returning to Poland and had suits specially made, but the bombing of Belgrade by the Germans quickly put a stop to that idea. Once the young prince regent Peter fled, there was political chaos and suddenly Belgrade felt very dangerous. My mother decided we should move to Italian-occupied Croatia.

We stayed in a lovely little seafront resort on the Adriatic coast that was occupied by Italians and Polish refugees. The Red Cross was stationed there looking after the refugees and my aunt was chosen to run the operation. This proved extremely complicated because her job was to get money from the Vatican through to Croatia, traversing a country that was now formally the enemy. Strangely, at this time, the Italian Army was totally against the Germans and the Fascists and we all enjoyed marvellous friendships and support from the Army, quite apart from everyone falling madly in love with the handsome Italian officers.

I learnt Italian and practised my English and the whole family would gather and listen to news from London. Often Churchill spoke on the radio and we would hang on his every word. To us he was like God himself and everything seemed to depend on his *parola divina*. When the Italians made peace with the Allies in 1943, they left all the occupied territories of Yugoslavia and liberated a tiny island called Krk. They advised us to move there because it would be safer than the mainland, where there was a lot of fighting amongst partisans. Very soon after we arrived with about a hundred other Poles, the Germans started bombing the island and then recaptured it. They ordered everyone to report morning and evening to the German officers on duty.

In the early hours of one morning they gave us all half an hour to take what we wanted and board a military ship. My mother asked the Germans where they were sending us and the German officer replied, 'You will be sent back to Poland because you are all disturbing military operations.' My mother asked, 'Do I have your word of honour as a German officer that we will be under Red Cross protection?' The officer replied, 'Yes.' Until this point, we had been getting by on mother's jewellery and living with a fisherman and his family in a little village on the island.

Distrustful of the German officer, my mother gave the fisherman a little lemon tree in a pot to take care of in our absence. Buried in the soil were the rest of her jewels. She knew that they simply would not last the trip in our hands to wherever we were going. We were transported to another island and then to Trieste. There we sat up through the night in the station, guarded by Italians. I decided I had to get word out to our friends and relations about where we were and what was happening, so I persuaded a soldier that I had a bad tummy ache and needed the loo. I was hoping that there would be someone inside who could help and sure enough, inside was an Italian female attendant.

I quickly scribbled a note on a piece of toilet paper explaining that the Germans were transporting us and I asked her to post it, which she did. We were first sent to Klagenfurt, a German prison in Austria. At Klagenfurt they isolated those below the age of sixteen and above the age of sixty, male and female. They claimed they would be going back to Poland. Then all the men were taken – guards came for them at three or four in the morning, screaming and shouting and banging the doors to frighten us.

The story only gets grimmer. My mother remembers:

The worst was when they took the children, because some of them were so little. I recall a child of two walking barefoot over the bare stones of the prison corridor, nappy trailing. It was November or December and there was such a silence. None of the children cried. None of the mothers cried. And the next day they put us into cattle carts. Nobody knew where we were going. We crossed Germany, avoiding all the stations that had been ruined by Allied bombs. We were guarded by Austrian paramilitaries, and even though none of us spoke German we were able to make ourselves understood. Several times, one Austrian suggested to us that we give him our jewels for safe keeping: 'If you take them with you, they are likely to be confiscated, but if you leave them with me I promise I will keep them safe.' I immediately asked my mother if we could test this out by giving him something small, but she said, 'Don't talk to these people or befriend them. You are always ready to talk to anybody and you are naive and stupid. For God's sake behave with some dignity towards the enemy.'

We arrived at Ravensbrück, which was 90 kilometres north of Berlin. It was the middle of the night. The camp guards opened the doors to the cattle car, yelling at us in their long boots and black coats, dogs growling, and they ordered the screaming men and women out. They arranged us in fives and marched us through frost and snow to the camp. Every guard had a pistol and a dog on a lead. The swastika was everywhere and now I understood what the symbol meant. We were led through an enormous gate and into a big sort of hole: 'When daylight comes, we will wash you. You bring with you all the diseases of the world and we can't have them here in our camp.'

That night we were ordered to lie on the floor and rest. Everything became quiet and as people lay down, I had no idea what was going to happen next. I couldn't see any guards, so I pulled out a cigarette and lit up. Suddenly, whoom – a huge punch to my face, right there in the dark. The cigarette went flying and I started to bleed. I hadn't seen the female guards lying in wait in the blackness. 'What do you think this is, a health spa, you Polish swine?' 'Ah, here we go,' I thought. I was deaf as a post for three days.

The next day they started examining us to make sure we weren't holding anything back. Soon we had nothing, not even a comb or a toothbrush. After showering us off, they gave out the uniforms. They didn't bother to give us the right sizes. It was a grotesque sight – tall people in miniature trousers and small people wearing oversized tops like dresses. Placed in so-called 'quarantine' for a month, we were given a thin soup made from potato peelings, in which occasionally a horse's eye would float to the surface.

At the beginning we couldn't eat it, but hunger changed all that. If you had been in the camp for a few years, you wouldn't have batted an eyelid at the seemingly constant presence of lice and fleas; the place was crawling with them and it disgusted me. We would spend hours looking for them and killing them, but the minute you went next door you'd catch them once again. Everyone started to get ill and the guards would insist on counting us at least three times a day – it was purely to annoy us. Everyone had to learn his or her number in German.

When we arrived there were about 26,000 of us, but by the time I left there were 500,000 or so prisoners – it was gigantic. Gradually they put us to work. My job seemed rather pointless, shovelling coal from one pile to the other. It was freezing cold; we had no gloves or shoes, just these wooden clogs. If you stopped work for just a few minutes they would set the dogs on you. Eventually they chose me for one of the metal factories, making parts for V1 and V2 bombs.

I would be given a piece of rusty iron and from it I had to make screws of different sizes and lengths. It was very hard, because the sharp iron would cut my fingers to shreds. You really had to know what you were doing. I worked the nightshift, which was particularly tough because there were fewer people around and there was no time to rest for even a minute. During the day it was hard to sleep, as the prisoners would be cleaning the camp. The windows were opened wide, which made it virtually impossible to sleep on account of the cold.

I was constantly worried about my mama, who was far too weak to stand it all. She immediately landed in the hospital and people warned me, 'If somebody stays in there too long and doesn't work, they will be considered a burden to the German state and will be cremated.' We could see the crematorium in Ravensbrück and we knew the Germans were burning Jews and gypsies there. Sometimes, walking around, you would trip or stumble against a piece of human bone. I continued my work in the factory and began to get to know my fellow workers.

They were mainly Ukrainian and Russian women and we used to listen to each other's stories. They were simple girls who had been sent to work for German farmers, then sent to the camps for misdemeanours, like stealing a sausage or sleeping with the farmer's son. The girls wanted to know what life as an aristocrat in Poland was like. At first I started to speak candidly about it, but then I got bored and started inventing things, embellishing the stories with fairy tales. I told them I grew up in a place where horses had golden shoes and our teeth were repaired with diamond fillings; every morning we would bathe in donkey's milk and rose petals. The girls loved to listen and in return they sang Russian songs. They sang in perfect harmony and were extremely musical.

I taught them 'It's a Long Way to Tipperary'; neither the Germans nor anybody else knew how completely anti-German the song was. On the contrary, our guards were very pleased we appeared to be enjoying our work so much. The organisation of the camp was meticulous. Each nation had a sort of underground network, which told us what to do and what not to do. In the factory, they explained that the first thing you had to do was to change the measurements of parts, which meant taking a very heavy hammer and banging the parts several times.

Consequently, when the arms were produced in their entirety nothing ever fitted together properly. These were V1s and V2s – extremely dangerous – and of course, they had to have a perfect finish. But what the Germans didn't realise was that once the weapons were assembled a couple of months later, they wouldn't fit together at all.

In early 1945 we started to hear rumours that Germany was being defeated by the Allies, but we didn't know how far away they were. Then one day a car arrived. A man got out and walked round the camp smoking American cigarettes. My friend told me to go and ask him what was going on, so I did. I must have looked a dreadful sight. I was very weak and I couldn't even find a comb but I did approach him and spoke to him in French. On my sleeve was the P indicating I was a Polish political prisoner. 'Tell me your name. How is it you speak such good French?' he said. When I told him, he remarked: 'I know your family very well. My name is Ankh Kroner. I'm Swedish and I'm Count Bernadotte's secretary.' I knew everything about Bernadotte's mission to evacuate the camps.

Red Cross ambulances took us to Lübeck. At the Red Cross centre, masked workers resembling astronauts in their white plastic uniforms, boots and gloves greeted us. They were scared of catching our illnesses but they were hospitable and friendly behind their masks. The next morning we crossed the Baltic Sea to Trelleborg, where we were greeted by an orchestra playing the national anthem of each group of arriving prisoners.

When people ask me how I managed to survive the camp and emerge unscathed by nightmares and hatred and bitterness, it is because of my firm belief that you can suffer almost anything at the hands of your enemies. Where an enemy makes you suffer, it's normal. He has to destroy you and you have to survive. But it's very, very difficult to suffer something from somebody you consider a friend. When a friend or lover betrays you, there is nothing worse.

That is the end of my mother's account of what happened to her at the hands of the Germans. But sometimes it isn't just memories that come back to haunt you. One day, when she had lived in England for a good couple of years, she was in Kensington, not far from the Polish Hearth Club, when a shocking thing happened. This is how she recounted it:

I was walking down Gloucester Road when I noticed a very well-dressed woman walking on the pavement in front of me. Her walk reminded me of something very vividly. I couldn't make out exactly who she was but I felt I knew her somehow. Eventually my curiosity got the better of me and I sped up, walked past her and took a good look. Suddenly it dawned on me who the woman was. She was one of the *Aufseherin* at Ravensbrück. A very beautiful woman, it was said that she had been a lion tamer before joining the camp guards. I don't know if it was true but she was certainly very agile, with an amazing figure and very distinctive catlike movements. She had been one of the cruellest guards, who would think nothing of beating you, kicking you, killing you. She had wielded absolute power and now there she was, walking next to me on Gloucester Road.

I thought of alerting people in the street, then catching

her and taking her to the police station, but I made a choice there and then. It's only now I realise why I just let her slip through my fingers: I simply didn't want to be involved in all that any more. I had a new life in England, which I wanted to continue living in peace.

CHAPTER 18

NO LONGER MY DIESEL, MY DEN

Having just lost both my dear parents within three weeks of each other and with my marriage in a very rocky state, 1996 was going to be an incredibly hard year. I used to ask my mother's advice about everything. She was always interested in the minutiae of my life and of course passionate about her first grandchild, my daughter Lara. It also made me realise how irreplaceable, unique and important family is. I am so lucky to have two wonderful sisters and a brother, and this time of turmoil brought me even closer to all of them.

Things at Sheepcote were going from bad to worse. Dennis had been wonderful and supportive after the death of my mother. In his own way he had loved her, but he had no such affection for my father. His feelings about family in general were nothing like as strong or involved as mine, though he was fairly close to some of his sisters. The scale and depth of the pain of losing both parents was a closed book to him, which made it very hard for me.

I had found out that contrary to what he had told me about him and Fiona being finished, he was still seeing her in secret. Any trust that remained was now completely gone. My daughter was then sixteen, still at boarding school and not having a good time. She was being badly bullied, not least because we were spread all over the papers. One of the great sadnesses of my life is that I didn't pull her out of there a lot earlier. But it was just at the time of her GCSEs and things at home were so volatile and unpredictable that I finally decided she was in a safer place at school.

In the autumn of that year, in Dzików, the first gathering of my mother's clan, the Tarnowskis, was due to take place in the house where she was born. This was something she had been so looking forward to and planning for. Sadly it was too late. She had missed it by just a few months.

The whole of my family was going: it would be a gathering of at least four generations and my sisters and brother decided it would be a lovely idea to take some of my mother's ashes and bury them beneath a weeping willow in the grounds of this family house that had meant so much to her. I begged Dennis to come with me. My sister Gaba was bringing her husband and her children from America, my brother Andrew was bringing his wife and children, and of course countless cousins and aunts and uncles from all over the world were going to be there.

Dennis had no interest in it. He said something like,

'I don't want to be surrounded by old Polish cabbages.' So that was that. I certainly did not want him to come with that attitude because this was going to be a very special and nostalgic journey.

We were all due to meet in Krakow for a reunion dinner in a small, family-run hotel. My mother's younger brother would be officiating. Everyone was excited as we took off from Gatwick. I was going to be sharing a room with both my sisters and my aunt Marys.

On the evening of our arrival we all got dressed up and assembled in the large function room attached to the hotel. There were about sixty of us. We had a sumptuous meal with free-flowing vodka and a wonderful welcome from a traditionally dressed folk group singing and dancing the songs we had learnt at Polish school all those years ago.

Across a crowded room I caught sight of a very handsome gentleman who shortly afterwards was introduced to me as a cousin, albeit a fairly distant one. He was called Wladek. There was definitely a frisson – the first time I had had any feelings of that sort since meeting Dennis. Over the next five days we did a lot of talking and gentle flirting. To me it was a totally new sensation and it lightened my mood and raised my spirits to know that I was still able to have those feelings for a man.

The itinerary for our few days was very full, with speeches and meals, visits to museums and cemeteries, mass outings and picnics in the woods and piano recitals. I felt myself more and more drawn to this man, and since he was from the same background there was, besides the physical attraction, an unspoken understanding I had never experienced before. It was almost as if my mother had sent him as a sort of rescue. It had always been a dream of hers that one of her daughters would end up with a Polish gentleman.

In a break between all the organised happenings my sisters and my brother and I held an intimate little ceremony as we laid her ashes in the gardens of the house she was born in. It was very moving to be able to lay her to rest in the country she so loved.

Wladek was a few years younger than me, separated from his wife and with two adopted children. He was easy to talk to and a marvellous dancer. He lived on a large country estate about an hour from Krakow and seemed not to have much in the way of a job. He had built his house with his own hands and it was his pride and joy. Though we did flirt and it was obvious that our feelings were mutual, we were adamant that nothing could happen for now.

Things at home were so uncertain and I was in a low and insecure state, so I certainly wasn't going to throw myself into a rebound scenario, but those few days did make me feel there could be light at the end of the tunnel and we decided that we would keep in touch by letter. I was completely honest with him about my marriage and told him that I still had hope that maybe things could be rescued.

When I got back I was full of all that had happened and tried to share it with Dennis. He was less than interested, but amongst the photos I showed him there were a few of me and Wladek. They were totally innocent but he immediately pounced on them and started accusing me of having an affair. I told him the truth that yes, there was an attraction, but nothing had happened. He didn't believe me.

I tried to say to him many times that I wanted us to mend things but that I needed to regain my trust in him. I had to make a decision. Either I was going to hang on and somehow turn a blind eye to the drinking and possibly to more of his infidelities or I would have to go. I just thanked God that my mother was no longer alive to see this. I was at the end of my tether.

Then came the three nights in close succession which sort of made my mind up for me, when the drinking led to physical attacks, which were terrifying – full of hate, anger, jealousy and aggression. This was not the Dennis I had known and loved so very much.

On the final evening, when he smashed photos of my family and came at me with a piece of glass, I ran out of the house into the night.

At the time, I was playing Lady Macbeth in an open-air production in Stafford. I just jumped into the car in the early hours of the morning and drove to my Stafford hotel, having left Dennis in his extremely drunken state. I was horrified when, several hours later, he turned up, having driven himself. Only his guardian angels working overtime saw to it that he did not kill himself or someone else. He smashed the lock and came into my bedroom, knelt down by the bed and came out with a long, tearful stream of apology.

I decided this really could not go on any longer so when the play's run finished I went to stay with my brother in London and over the following few weeks tried to work out what would be the best thing to do. My family were as supportive as always and I moved from pillar to post for a short time before being offered a room with a dear friend in Battersea, which I accepted.

I had never really spent any significant time on my own. From living at home I went to sharing flats with various groups of friends at drama school and then to cohabiting with my first serious boyfriend, the flamboyant and eccentric Pavlik Stooshnoff. Then came Brian Deacon, who was to become my first husband, and then sixteen years with Dennis.

So, at the end of 1996, at the ripe old age of nearly fifty, I found myself alone for the first time, with the knowledge that I was going to have to learn to cater financially, emotionally and practically for myself and my sixteen-year-old daughter. Both of us had been through the mill in the final few years with Dennis, both of us were traumatised and exhausted physically and emotionally, and the view of this empty, lonely road was a frightening prospect, not least because of the still huge interest and often antagonistic attention from the press.

There were some friends of ours whose loyalties were understandably divided – they had known Dennis a long time – but there were also others who had been very close to me and had seemingly abandoned me. I thank God for my wonderful, supportive siblings who have always been there for me through thick and thin, a handful of lifelong friends and my first husband, who, even after the awful heartache I had caused him, was there to lend me a helping hand as well as always being totally steadfast in his love and support for our daughter.

It was a horrible time. We would have to move out of the house that had become very dear to me and of course, even more important, very dear to my daughter Lara. I had got so used to living in the country and loved being surrounded by green fields and woods and fresh air, and it had been her home for most of her life. My daughter and I had made good friends in the area. The Venns, our next-door neighbours, were particularly difficult to leave. They had always been with us, in good times and bad, and their children were some of Lara's closest friends.

Paddy Hopkirk, the famous rally driver, and his wife Jenny were always staunch and loyal and so, of course, was my dearest friend Michèle Clarke. But I knew I couldn't afford a house in that neck of the woods and my daughter wanted to go to nursing college, so the only option was to move back to London.

I didn't have any money, not even enough for a deposit for a lease on a rented place, so I ended up staying with my Battersea friends the Walfords for several months. It was a hard and frightening time. My daughter wasn't enjoying boarding school, but in a sense this horrible period was a vindication of my decision to send her – at least she wasn't around while I was going through my ordeals and feeling so traumatised.

I didn't come out well financially from the split with Dennis. The economy was in recession and our house wasn't easy to sell, and when we did finally find a buyer it went for well below its true market value. Dennis accused me publicly of robbing him because I asked for half the value of the house, which was rightly mine. He still had a huge outstanding debt set against the house for the film he had made in Chicago. He thought I should pay half that debt. I refused. So there was another, even more bitter battle.

I knew he had private pensions and other large sums of money put aside on the advice of all the people who were attached to his manager and agent, and of course all his working life he had earned much more than me. When lawyers got involved they tried to persuade me to hit him hard in many other areas of future earnings. I never did that. I simply asked for my fair share from the house.

Finally and generously he did allow me to have the French

house, which I had to sell. We had spent a lot of money on it – far more than we planned – and by the time we were falling apart as a couple it was only half done, and that's how it stayed. Sadly, that had also gone way down in value and it pained me to part with it. That place had been a sort of retirement dream; it turned out to be a pipe dream. But the money I got for it enabled me to buy the small house I still live in today.

In the meantime I found a little terraced house in Chiswick to rent for a year while we were struggling with the divorce proceedings and this at least gave me a bit of breathing space and some privacy, though the press were still very much on my case. I chose Chiswick because it was near my youngest sister; it was leafy and green and near the river and close to the M4 going out of London. It turned out to be a good choice.

In 2012 Dennis did an hour-long television interview with Piers Morgan. In it he admitted that he had hit me, something he had publicly denied for fifteen years and which I had been called a liar for even suggesting. So it was something of a relief to have it out in the open but it was a shock that he would allow himself to be exposed in that way. Given the nature of these *Life Stories* interviews he must have known it was going to come up. Perhaps he felt that in the great scheme of things it wasn't a major issue.

Anyway, he said he had a reason for doing it or at least a good excuse: 'The problem with strong, intelligent women is that they can argue well. And if there is a time where you can't get a word in … and I … I lashed out. I couldn't end the argument.' He certainly wasn't apologetic. He seemed not to understand that it was no excuse and that hitting a woman is seen nowadays as inexcusable.

When he talked to Morgan after the recording he said, 'I think that went pretty well, it was good to finally set the record straight.' Later Morgan wrote: 'What's extraordinary is that he didn't seem to have a clue that what he'd said might be remotely controversial.'

Actually, I don't think I was cleverer than him. I might be more educated but not cleverer. Certainly, when most of the confrontations happened, I wasn't drunk and he was, so I was more on top of things and I would not walk away without asking (not to say demanding to know) why he was doing these things to destroy us.

Having read quite a lot since about co-dependence and alcohol, I now understand that when someone's in that drunken state you shouldn't push for explanations because they just get more and more intolerant, more and more aggressive and more and more 'Sod it, I don't have to explain anything, this is my house and I will behave how I want and you have no right to demand.' How well I remember him yelling that kind of thing at me.

When he said to Morgan, 'Yeah, all right, I must have hit her, she had a black eye the following day,' he was probably mouthing what he thought a rough-diamond *Minder*-type character would say. I think he was genuinely sorry and scared on the few occasions when there was physical violence.

And again, Dennis was never violent when he was sober. It was not part of his character. It was only the drink that created it. After a big session, whether it was staying out hours and hours after he said he was coming back, or driving when he was way over the limit, or probably both, he would always come back on the attack, knowing he was in the wrong.

The second time he hit me I said, 'If this ever happens again, I'm leaving,' and when you say something like that you've got to stand by it. My feelings for him had always been very strong, and even during all of the bad things we went through, the love was always there. I felt tremendous sadness and disappointment and fear that here was something else that was going to collapse, was going to finish. I wasn't strong enough (or weak enough) to carry on the way we were, waiting for good times but knowing they would always be followed by bad times.

I wasn't willing to accept that the only way that we were going to continue was just to allow Dennis to be Dennis, addicted to drinking and golf. I know of so many relationships where one partner accepts a rock-bottom modus vivendi which allows things to go on but unhappily and unfulfilled. I was scared of losing sight of who I was and for a long time towards the end it felt like walking on eggshells.

I never knew who was coming back in the early hours of the morning, Dr Jekyll or Mr Hyde. It was frightening and I was no longer willing to put myself, let alone my daughter, through it. This was no longer my Diesel, my Den.

CHAPTER 19

A SAD ENDING

Throughout these early times by myself after leaving Dennis I was in regular contact with my friend Wladek in Poland, who was supportive and warm and caring, and whenever I had some free time I went over there or he came over here, and I must say that was a huge consolation.

In my life with Dennis we had been very comfortable financially. Suddenly money, or the lack of it, was something I had to think about alone. Work was sporadic and bills and all the minutiae of daily life were my sole responsibility.

No longer being frightened of which Dennis was coming home at nights was a relief, but being alone and lonely was a big mountain to climb. There were many times when I thanked God that my parents were no longer alive to see how things had changed.

The press, of course, quickly learnt Dennis and I were splitting up and I was shadowed and followed constantly. It was painful and frightening. I was still in a very low mental state and I refused to say anything to them, I made no comment at all for several months, but whenever I was in male company – once even with my brother – there were snappers trying to put me in an awkward position. So finally, on the advice of a lawyer and my agent, I decided I would speak briefly to one of the papers and quite gently tell my side of the story.

My daughter was home from boarding school on an exeat. I had arranged to speak on the Saturday with a journalist who had been recommended to me as gentle. On the Friday evening quite late at night I was in the kitchen clearing up after some friends had been round for supper when the doorbell went. It was about eleven o'clock. My daughter answered the door to a lady with a large bouquet of flowers and a bottle of champagne who told her she was an old school friend of mine, so of course she let her in.

She showed her into the kitchen. I didn't recognise her – I had never seen her before in my life. She immediately started by saying how she admired me for being so brave and that she knew what it was like to have been in a destructive relationship and so on. I kept saying, 'Sorry, who are you?' And I added that I had never said that I had been in a destructive relationship. She just kept saying I could trust her and she was on my side. Finally she admitted that she was from a tabloid newspaper.

I didn't discuss anything with her or answer any questions. Furiously and in no uncertain terms I told her to get the hell out of my house with her flowers and champagne.

The following weekend there was a horrible article, using words and terminology that had not come out of my mouth, but of course it put the kibosh on the interview I had agreed to do with the journalist from another weekend paper. It never happened. And worst of all was the headline, calling Dennis a wife-beater.

On the advice of my lawyers I went straight to the Press Complaints Commission, accusing the woman of invasion of privacy. I lost the case because she said she had been invited into the house. Well, yes, she had, because she lied about who she was.

Understandably this made the situation between Dennis and me much worse. All sorts of people started coming out of the woodwork defending him and accusing me of being a liar. I had never called him a 'wife-beater' but no one from his side believed me. I decided it was important to set the record straight so I did an interview with a Sunday paper saying that on a few occasions when he was very drunk he had lashed out at me, but I also said that when sober there was not an aggressive bone in his body. He strenuously denied he had ever lifted his hand to me and continued to do so in press interviews. In his memoirs, published in 2000 he did say he had 'lashed out three times' but for the next dozen years I was treated as if I was lying.

His accusations and the comments from his camp harmed me, my family and my career. I was branded the wrongdoer and an opportunist only interested in furthering my own ambitions. It was hurtful and completely untrue. We had been very much in love and, for a long time, very happy. It was cruel that it all had to finish in such a horrible and vitriolic way. To this day I have not set eyes on him. I try now to remember all the wonderful times and would love before the end of my time to somehow make our peace.

I began to pull myself together. There was some work coming in and I had to think about making a stable home for my daughter and learning to live on my own. The sun began to filter through the greyness. Meanwhile, contact with my friend Wladek in Poland was becoming more regular and important. Just after Christmas I had to go over to deal with some family business. I would spend time with him and see if that initial spark led to anything. Dennis already had a new lady in his life and things with the press had quietened down.

I arrived in a snow-covered Krakow shortly before the New Year and after a few days with Krysia I met up with Wladek, who had invited me to come for the New Year festivities in his house in the country. It was magical. He was a real gentleman, kind and thoughtful and warm and welcoming. His friends were delightful and I loved his mother, who was an opera-singing teacher. There were romantic walks in the snow-covered forests and family evenings round a roaring log fire. And then finally a few days just the two of us up in the mountains of Zakopane visiting friends of his, and a tentative love began to bloom.

My mother had always said that class and a similar social background are important, and I had always argued against it. But suddenly I could see what she meant. There was a level and ease of communication I had not experienced before. Of course having family in common helped, we both spoke Polish and, very importantly, alcohol was not part of daily life.

Gradually I got back my faith in myself. I began to see that there was a way forward, that this was not the end of my life. I realised I was now in charge and that only I could make things better. I had been brought up with the idea that happiness is something that can only happen when you are part of a happy couple. Somehow I had messed up twice already. Maybe it was time for a rethink, time to realise that actually happiness isn't something that comes just from being with someone else, that maybe it's a state of personal contentment and internal peace and knowing and accepting who you are and liking or even loving yourself. My happiness was my own responsibility.

Since I had been renting in Chiswick and liked it, I started to look for something to buy there. It was a convenient location for me in many ways and it had a caring, village atmosphere. I saw many properties before I finally found something that was within my price range – a smallish terraced house in a nice street. It had the right sort of accommodation for a teenage daughter to have her own space and did not need a lot of structural work. I had a team of Polish workmen who agreed, at a considerably reduced price, to transform the kitchen area, which was small, old-fashioned and dark. There was also a loft conversion with a big enough bed-sittingroom to make my daughter feel a bit more self-contained. I am still here fifteen years down the line. It's cosy, safe and it houses no bad memories. It's my own home and my nest.

In summer 1997 I was offered a wonderful part in the Chichester season. The play was *Our Betters* by Somerset Maugham, starring Kathleen Turner. In the countryside nearby I found myself a nice little flat owned by Alexandra Bastedo, attached to a gorgeous animal sanctuary with dogs and cats and donkeys and pigs. For a dedicated animal lover like me it was a glorious little haven – two months of being back in the country. And I was in a wonderful play with a wonderful cast. Heaven! Wladek was going to be coming over for a whole month and I had a perfect place for Lara to come and spend time with me.

Kathleen Turner was a big Hollywood film star and a terrific actress and the play generated a lot of interest. She and I became quite close. I had a complicated dance routine to perform in the second act of the show in a very beautiful long period gown. One afternoon during the matinée I got tangled up in my train and fell rather badly, twisted my ankle and had to miss a couple of shows. Sadly, the understudy had not been well rehearsed and when I came back into the show I was summoned into Kathleen's dressing room. All the other cast were very sympathetic because my foot was still bandaged and painful, but Kathleen snapped at me, 'Don't you ever, ever let me down again like that.' Flattering, in a way, I suppose.

I had first met Wladek in 1996 but our serious relationship didn't start until many months later and it lasted for six years, though of course we were apart for the vast majority of that time, me in London and him in Poland. A year into our relationship we both thought it would be marvellous to go away together. Neither of us had much money, but I remembered I had two BA Club Class return tickets to anywhere in the world. They were given to me instead of payment for a couple of jobs I did for British Airways and they had been sitting there unused.

We decided, or perhaps I did, that we would go to South America, starting in Colombia with a visit to my beloved drama school friend Don MacIver, who was teaching English and drama in Bogotá. We had a terrific time with him and his boyfriend Jairo in the city and at their *finca* in the country. This was a long holiday, so it was onwards to Peru, a country full of wonders, some, like Machu Picchu and Lake Titicaca, famous to everybody, others unknown to us till we found them. We went into the Amazonian rainforest and saw less in the way of animals than I'd hoped for. Some of our best wildlife experiences were with humans.

Our meeting with a high-up Amazonian chief didn't turn out quite as I'd expected. We were sitting in his tent when he arrived to meet us not in full regalia but naked apart from rather grubby, torn blue swimming trunks. He and I had no common language – my Spanish didn't stretch very far – but through our interpreter we managed quite a long conversation, mainly about how the role of Amazonian women had changed in recent years.

The chief announced that this was the most interesting conversation he had ever had with a woman so he was going to initiate me into a ceremony very few women experience. Wladek was pretty nervous about it but my attitude, as so often in my life, was 'yeah, why not?' A man appeared with two plastic bags, out of which the chief pulled a fantastic headdress of plumes and feathers from all sorts of exotic birds, and a heavy necklace of beads and claws; he also had a little canister – the sort of thing that film for cameras used to come in.

Our host opened it and asked me to hold out my hand, onto which he poured a greenish-whitish powder. Then he took some ash from the fire and mixed it in. And to my horror, and Wladek's even greater horror, he coughed and gobbed spit into my hand. Then, with his long filthy fingernails he moulded the stuff into a green wodge that looked like chewing gum and motioned me to open my mouth and put it in. In the circumstances it was not an optional request. He did the same with his wodge. We carried on chatting and within five minutes I had no feeling in my mouth and throat at all and a sensation of clarity and brightness in my head. Cocaine, no

With Leonard Rossiter in *Abel, Where Is Your Brother?*, 1974.

Playing Eskimo Nell alongside the funniest men in showbiz, Morecambe and Wise.

LEFT Five months pregnant, and still not showing, with Clive Arrindell in Noël Coward's *Design for Living*, 1979.

With the inimitable Les Dawson and Christopher Timothy in rehearsal for *Aladdin*, 1981.

LEFT John Inman as my secretary in *Take a Letter, Mr Jones*, 1981.

BELOW What a thrill to have been in the *Doctor Who* story 'Resurrection of the Daleks', playing Dr Styles alongside the Fifth Doctor, Peter Davison, 1984.

LEFT Playing Lady Macbeth in an open-air production at Stafford Castle, 1996, at a time of great turmoil at home.

BELOW This was just one of my rather beautiful costumes for Stephen Sondheim's *A Little Night Music.*

ABOVE *An Inspector Calls*, and the famous collapsing house, at the Garrick Theatre, 2001.

LEFT *84 Charing Cross Road*, 2004 – the happiest and best piece of theatre in recent years.

LEFT Playing the mother of a runaway child in a slightly under-rehearsed monologue!

BELOW The hugely successful *Calendar Girls* on tour in 2011.

ABOVE The Three Pussies: me, Jennie Jules and Tilly Blackwood, from *The Vagina Monologues*, 2011.

LEFT With my darling Papa.

Mama, crowned on her 70th, in Sheepcote.

With my special daughter, Lara.

With the light of my life, my grandson.

doubt, in its natural habitat. As for the chief's bodily fluids – I have lived to tell the tale.

On our last night in Peru the guide brought us a small container of what he said was the purest marijuana anywhere in the world. Wladek was against drugs of any kind but I thought it had to be worth a try. Bad call! It made me completely paranoid and it took all Wladek's powers of persuasion to get on to the plane back to Bogota. I was convinced it was going to crash. But we made it back. It had been a wonderful six weeks with a wonderful companion.

As the relationship with Wladek became more intense, there were often discussions as to where it was going. At first we talked about spending equal time together in Poland and in England but, if truth be told, I seemed to go over there much more than he came over here. Partly, of course, it was understandable. Though his English was pretty good, he felt like a fish out of water in this country and the possibility of him finding work over here was almost zero.

He had all his family and friends over there. I had all my family and friends plus a career over here. And though my Polish was better than his English it was still very difficult for me to contemplate moving there. Initially, speaking to other Polish actors, I naively believed that I could have a career of sorts in Poland. My Polish was fluent, albeit a bit old-fashioned, but I soon found out that unless there was a part which demanded a foreign-born Pole with a slight accent, actresses born in Poland would have priority, which is as it should be.

At the time Wladek had a beautiful house in the country about forty minutes from the centre of Krakow surrounded by 25 hectares of land, but no real job to speak of. He did a bit of work with mobile phones and computers and taught skiing in the winter months but really he was looking for something he could be passionate about and develop using his land. We came up with lots of suggestions together and in the end he decided to develop the land into a conference centre, the first of its kind in Poland. This would be a long and expensive process, and what was I going to do? Unless I went into teaching it was hard to imagine.

I loved Poland and I loved being with him but the idea of moving there full time would mean losing my new-found independence, leaving my daughter, who still needed me, separating myself from my family and friends and virtually giving up my career. It wasn't really an option. Now I sometimes wonder if I made the right decision.

CHAPTER 20

'HOW ABOUT DOING *CELEBRITY BIG BROTHER?*'

I was at the dentist's and I happened to say how wonderful I thought *Strictly Come Dancing* was and how I'd love to be on it and he said, 'Well, strangely enough, my wife is an agent. She looks after sports people mostly and she gets them into these programmes. Let's see what she can do.'

So I met up with her, a very beautiful, glamorous lady called Corinne, and she got in touch with *Strictly Come Dancing* but their quota was full for that particular series – they certainly weren't looking for anyone else to fill the 'slightly older woman' role.

'How do you feel about doing *Celebrity Big Brother?*' she asked. 'Not in a million years,' I replied, 'I think it's cruel and horrible and I couldn't possibly see myself doing it.'

'Well, hang on a second,' she said, 'let's talk about this. They pay better than *Strictly Come Dancing* and they guarantee to give a certain amount of money to your chosen charity, so why don't I arrange a meeting with them and we'll see where we go from there?'

I contacted my agent Paul Pearson and mentioned this to him and he said, 'Well, first of all, there'll be a slight problem with percentages because I'm your agent and if she gets you this job, she's going to expect agent's commission and I'm not sure if I'm happy about that.'

Oh well. I decided we could sort that out later if indeed there was a later. Corinne organised an initial meeting in Wembley with three of the producers. I knew very little about the programme because it wasn't something I watched. In hindsight it was pretty stupid not to have watched a lot more of it.

The producers were charming – very young and very discreet. They were seeing lots of people but three weeks later they came back and said, 'Yes, we would love to have you on the programme – how do you feel about it?' My agent had warned me, 'Watch out when they ask you about phobias and fears, because they will play on that. And when they ask you what you think the point of Big Brother is and what you think will be your greatest asset and your greatest problem in the house – think carefully about how you answer those questions, because it will arm Big Brother even further.' So I had been warned but the thing I now know about Big Brother is that nobody can warn you enough.

The point the producers stressed most was that if I agreed

to do the programme I was sworn to total secrecy. I wasn't allowed to tell anybody, not even my family, and if word leaked out I would lose my place. Then the money discussions started and my fee was indeed pretty large. But even more of a carrot was the promise that 16 per cent of the monies made by the public interaction through texting, or emailing or phoning during the voting-out process would be divided up between the celebrities for their favourite charities. They said it would be at least £60,000 per celebrity for their charity. So that was what finally swung it.

There wasn't a lot happening for me work-wise at the time. Paul, my agent, was now very keen on it. It was one of the most popular things on television. I quizzed him about whether a real actress had been on it before, because in the few snippets I'd seen, it was all 'celebrities' and people from the world of sport and pop. I was a bit worried about that. I couldn't see it furthering my acting career. It was going to put me back on the map as far as the public was concerned, but that was a slightly double-edged sword. Did I want to be known for going into a reality TV show?

Anyway, my agent was persuasive and the money was obviously very enticing. But truly – believe this if you will – what appealed to me most of all was this promise of an enormous amount of money for me to give to my charities. The two agents split the 20 per cent between them and they were both happy with that.

The whole money aspect of it was great for a gig that lasted only three weeks and it didn't matter whether you were the first person to be voted out, you would still get your payment. Unless of course you chose to leave the house of your own volition – then you would forfeit it, supposedly.

There were about three weeks before it was due to start. I began to get terrible collywobbles about all the rules and regulations. For a start, I wasn't allowed to talk to anybody about it at all and I certainly stuck to that promise until three days before I went in. And you're told what you're allowed to pack, with a whole list of dos and don'ts. You were allowed to take in two hundred cigarettes and two bottles of booze, either wine, beer or champagne; no writing materials; obviously no mobile phones; no watches; no pens; no games of any sort; no magazines; no books; no knitting – nothing you could possibly use to occupy your time.

This came as a bit of a shock. I knew I wasn't allowed to take in watches and mobile phones. But I thought writing materials, pens and maybe some sort of handiwork would be allowed. However, I did win one tiny battle. I told them I was a Buddhist and chanted every day so could I have permission to take in my little booklet of prayers, plus my little Tibetan bell? And they said yes.

And medication – one wasn't allowed to take in headache pills or anything like that. That was in the rules but later I found out that for some people, the rules were flexible in various directions, particularly concerning medication. So then came the agonising over packing. Does one look glamorous? Does one look comfortable? How many outfits is one supposed to pack? How warm is it going to be in there? How cold is it going to be in there? What are the toilet facilities? I knew nothing about any of these things. I kept my agent up half the night with questions on the phone.

I told my daughter about it three days before I was due to go and swore her to secrecy. She said, 'Go for it, Mum.' And I dropped a note in to three neighbours saying the house was going to be empty for possibly three weeks, or it might only be three days, and I'm going into the Big Brother house. And a little girl from down the road called Ella who was only about eight or nine came on the morning I was going to be picked up and dropped an envelope through the letterbox with a good-luck charm bracelet and a message: 'Please wear this, it will protect you.' It was incredibly sweet of her and I did wear it all the way through.

A blacked-out limo came to pick me up with a very non-communicative minder. No conversations. It certainly wasn't jolly or relaxed. I do get nervous about things but this was a completely different nervousness – fear of the totally unknown. We arrived, finally, after about an hour's journey and we were met by people with scarves round their faces and walkie-talkies. I felt as if I'd been arrested. I was smuggled through various side doors, so I couldn't see anybody else who was arriving at the same time. And then I was taken up into a bedroom in this Holiday Inn-type hotel. There was a huge flask of coffee and sandwiches. My mobile phone and watch were taken away from me. There was nothing in the room that told you what time it was.

Then they unpacked my suitcase. All my clothes were allowed but everything was itemised. All my toiletries were allowed but everything that had a name or product information had to be blanked out with tape. It took about two and a half hours to pack everything into a Big Brother suitcase. There was any amount of hanging around, any number of cups of black coffee.

At the end of the afternoon I was completely wired and shaking like a leaf. By the time I was led back into the blacked-out car with my suitcase it was pretty dark. I hadn't had much to eat and I had smoked like a chimney so I had the beginnings of a really bad nervous headache and was literally quivering with fear.

I was driven to the Big Brother house. There were people standing on corners whispering into walkie-talkies. I was shoved through a side door into a tiny room, where I was left alone for about half an hour, and then in came a gentleman who was introduced by one of the walkie-talkie chaps as a psychoanalyst or psychiatrist. I had to spend an hour with him and at the end of the session I was informed that should I require his services for a further four to six weeks after the programme had finished he was at my disposal, with the tab picked up by the production company.

He asked how was I feeling and was I terribly nervous and how did I think I would function in a situation where I was virtually locked in. And of course, one didn't know whether this was being listened in to, whether he was wired for sound. I wasn't wearing a mike yet. It was a very bland little room, with just two chairs and a sink and nothing was offered to eat or drink. He wanted to know whether I ever suffered from depression, did I have any particular phobias, how did I get on with strangers and did I prefer the company of men or women.

I tried to ask him about the sorts of thing to expect, without success. I answered all his questions honestly but the one thing I was secretive about was my hearing problem. I did at that time wear one hearing aid and Big Brother promised me that they wouldn't reveal this or photograph it, and they stuck to their promise, thank God.

The shrink said to me, 'You realise you will be wearing a microphone at all times, which you can take off at night, but there is a microphone above your bed.' So then you start to get worried about the various bodily noises that might happen in the night when you're asleep. He asked if I thought I would be adversely affected by people voting me out, and how would I feel if I was the first person to be voted out. And did I want to win? It didn't really seem very important to me at the time, the winning part of it. The taking part seemed much more important.

They weren't giving anything away. And they made no attempt to be particularly warm or put you at your ease. The whole idea was to get you really tense with excitement and nerves before you actually appeared. I wasn't told whether I would be first in, or second, or third, or fourth, or last, just that at some point I would be picked up by one of the guys with a walkie-talkie and taken in a car. I would have headphones put on my head, so I couldn't hear anything, and I wouldn't see anything because the windscreens would be blacked out. The car would stop, the driver would get out and open my door and as I came out there would be a bank of photographers on the right-hand side and a bank of photographers on the left-hand side and I had to stand and be photographed for a minute on either side.

Davina McCall, the show's presenter, would come to get me and there would be a short interview then I would go into the house. So far it had been a whole day of almost total silence apart from the hour's conversation with the psychoanalyst. I was unbelievably hyped up on coffee and cigarettes and incredibly nervous and I had no idea what was going to happen.

I got into the car and the minder was again sitting beside me and there was no conversation whatsoever and the headphones were clamped on to my head, so I couldn't hear. It was a short drive – maybe a minute, probably less – and then he took my headphones off as the door opened and the barrage of sound was just unbelievable. All the supporters screaming and yelling and shouting – plus these long banks of photographers – four, five, six deep, all with their flashes going off. I was wearing fairly high heels and it was a grid walk and my knees were trembling, and my voice was trembling, and I was trembling all over – absolutely petrified, but excited as well, of course.

It was either like death row or like being on a red carpet at a huge premiere in Los Angeles, or both. There was an amazing feeling of euphoria because you were being photographed and screamed at by all these people, in a positive way. And then Davina. It was so comforting to feel a warmth and a welcoming hug from her. She announced my name and there was a short interview and she gave me a hug and whispered, 'Good luck.' I'm sure she did it to everybody, but it seemed personal and the physical contact was much needed, particularly with another woman.

I walked up this incredible staircase into the gaping eye of Big Brother, again with no idea what to expect, all the time praying that my heel wouldn't get stuck in the metal grid leaving me flat on my face.

I got up to the top of the stairs, the doors opened and I stepped in. The doors closed behind me and suddenly there was complete silence. I knew I was probably on camera because we were told that there were cameras everywhere. Some of them were visible and some of them were invisible. I walked down this staircase. There was another door. I opened it.

Inside the Big Brother *house/prison. From left: Pete Burns, Chantelle, George Galloway, me and Faria, with Maggot in the background.*

CHAPTER 21

ALL ABOUT MY HOUSEMATES

I was startled by all the bright colours and how glamorous the place looked, but when I looked a bit more closely I saw that it was all ticky-tacky and temporary. I think the US basketball star Dennis Rodman was already in there. He was a bit terrifying to look at – hugely tall, covered in tattoos and with piercings all over his face.

There was Faria Alam, a very beautiful girl who was one of Sven-Göran Eriksson's girlfriends, and Maggot, a pop singer with a group called Goldie Lookin Chain that I'd never heard of, very young. And Traci Bingham, a beautiful actress from *Baywatch* with an amazing figure. And I think the glamour model Jodie Marsh was already in there, along with Michael Barrymore.

That was quite a relief. I had never worked with him but of course I knew who he was, enjoyed his performances and greatly admired some of his TV shows. Recently the papers had been full of stories about the young man who'd been found dead in his swimming pool after a party at his house. Michael was overexcited and keen to impress. I was glad to see him. Immediately I was offered a glass of champagne. I'm not very good with champagne, it gives me a headache, but on this occasion I thought I had to be in there with everybody else.

The next in was Pete Burns, and that I will never forget. I didn't know who this extraordinary person was, with full make-up, amazing wig, beautifully dressed and scary – there was something really frightening about him. He had a career as a singer and songwriter but that wasn't what mattered. His personality and his energy took over the room instantly. Then I think it was Preston, a young pop star who, again, I didn't know. And then the left-wing politician George Galloway and I thought, oh good, finally somebody I might be able to talk to.

Obviously I knew who he was and I had followed his War on Want work. I thought of him as always fighting for victims and the underdog and I'd been impressed by him. He and Michael Barrymore were two people I thought I would be able to connect with. And then last in, I think, was Chantelle. The producers said she was a singer but none of us knew who she was or what she had done. In the end there were eleven of us. Also, some days later, when we were established in there – I was going to say settled, but we were never settled – we had a surprise guest. And who would that have been? Sir Jimmy Savile of course.

Within a very short time of everybody arriving, you hear,

'This is Big Brother.' I immediately got the impression that George Galloway and Pete Burns were completely in control of the situation. They didn't seem to show any nerves whatsoever. George was very friendly to me. Pete Burns was, I don't quite know how to explain it, slightly supercilious, and Barrymore was doing his usual performing. The others were much younger, apart from Dennis Rodman, so they sort of stuck together.

We were offered food. And then the dormitory was unlocked and for the first time I saw that we were all going to be sleeping in one room. They were single beds, and rather boxy single beds, set around a long rectangular space and every bed had a mirror above it. In fact, the whole wall was covered in mirrors. So we immediately knew that behind the mirrors were cameras. And hanging above every bed was a microphone. There was very little storage space – you had two pull-out drawers underneath each bed and a bedside cabinet.

People were unpacking their little overnight cases because the big suitcases hadn't been given to us yet and we were chatting and talking and generally trying to come to terms with our nerves. Then we all went back out to the main sitting/dining area and the outside bit was opened. Outdoors was a courtyard, and a sort of miniature swimming pool/hot tub thing and a seating area. We explored everything that could be explored and every so often Big Brother would come across on the microphone.

Then we came back in again and electronic shutters came down on all the windows, and when that happened you had no idea if it was day or night because you couldn't even see any daylight. And still, because it was a live programme, every so often you would hear the loudspeakers from outside and all the people screaming and shouting and some booing and some hooraying.

Groups started to form. Galloway and Michael Barrymore got together immediately and Barrymore was really playing the comic and had everybody's attention. When he was the star – and he was incredibly good at it – he was happy. When all of that palled a bit and he wasn't the centre of attention and he wasn't putting on funny accents and doing funny routines, he started to suffer.

George Galloway, in a way, began taking control. I noticed that very quickly he started calling us brothers and sisters – very Communist of him! Of all the people there, he was the one I was most interested in because I knew that he was a highly intelligent man, though I did think it was a bit strange that a Member of Parliament should come into a house like this rather than being out there doing whatever he was supposed to be doing.

I chose the end bed on the right-hand side of the sleeping room so I was nearest the bathroom, because I need to go to the loo quite often in the night. There was one toilet and one shower and then an open washbasin, with very tiny bits of space for your creams and toothbrush. At first I undressed either in the shower or in the toilet, but increasingly as time went by just in front of everybody. The youngsters had no problem about things like that. I always used to keep myself covered either with a towel or a robe.

I had something to eat and I think I had a brief conversation with George Galloway. In the bed next to me was Faria and next to her was Barrymore, then Galloway. They both warned us that they snored dreadfully, which was one advantage of wearing a hearing aid (I took it out at night and nobody was ever aware that I had it). Pete Burns slept at the end.

We were told by Big Brother that there were no cameras in either the shower or the toilet, which was true (I hope) but there were definitely microphones because they were able to pick up whispered conversations. I think I was one of the few people to crash early on the first night. Galloway, Pete Burns and Michael Barrymore stayed up for hours. It was never completely dark at night because they filmed right through so there was a strange green-tinged light that was on all the time. I think I managed to get a bit of sleep, but not a lot.

On the first morning we were woken up by dogs barking, Dobermans or Alsatians, really ferocious and incredibly loud. It could be six o'clock in the morning, it could be ten o'clock in the morning, because you have no idea of time and you have no idea of light, unless Big Brother allows you to see it. People got up in dribs and drabs and helped themselves to breakfast. The fridges and cupboards were really well stocked with amazing food and everything you could possibly want.

One of the first questions I asked the Big Brother team when I went for the interview was, 'Are we aware where the cameras are if they are filming us?' and they said no. There were some cameras on tracks that you became aware of, but the rest of them were hidden behind the walls or mirrors. So you knew you could be being filmed when you were scratching your bum or picking your nose or sitting blankly in the corner staring into space. It didn't matter which conversation you were having, everything was up for grabs filming-wise and of course you had to wear a microphone all the time and a little microphone pack. And every so often, if it got misplaced or you tried to cover it up to say something, Big Brother would come on overhead and say 'stop playing around with your microphone' or 'you've forgotten your microphone, go and put it on'.

On one particular night I woke some time in the early hours of the morning (I think) and the masking behind one of the mirrors facing right on to my bed had slipped and I could see a camera lens and just half a profile of the camera operator, with the camera pointing straight at me. I was under the covers and I watched him filming me, without him being aware of it. And very often at night when I couldn't sleep, what with the strange green light and Barrymore and Galloway snoring their heads off, and occasionally some of the younger ones flirting or sharing the same bed, I would think to myself, 'This is extraordinary. I can't believe I'm here, doing this, being filmed and people are watching me lying in bed doing nothing.'

And then every so often, individuals would be called into the diary room and Big Brother would ask questions like 'How are you feeling?' and 'What do you think of your fellow inmates?' And slowly, slowly you're getting into bits of conversation with people you'd thought you had nothing in common with. I didn't know who the youngsters were but everyone was being very pleasant with everybody else and I found a little corner in a room on the other side of the outside area, where I would take myself off for my Buddhist chanting morning and evening. I didn't know whether Big Brother was recording that.

Sometimes people joined me for a few minutes but I didn't feel any great need to explain what I was doing. It was just like praying. So I would ding my little bells and go through the gongyo. I think the first person who came to join me was Traci from *Baywatch* and she just said she found it calming and soothing.

All the young girls had hair extensions, so there were bits of hair lying all over the place in the sitting room and in the bedroom. We weren't allowed electric hairdryers so I had a battery-operated hair curler thing. After the first three or four hours in the day, after you'd had a few chats with everybody, you suddenly thought, 'My God, three weeks with nothing to do', unless you were into physical exercise – there was a small gym – or into conversation.

Then Big Brother called us all together and gave us our first task. We were to perform what we were best known for. I was given a piece of Shakespeare; the two young pop stars were obviously given pop songs; Barrymore was given a bit of light entertainment; George Galloway had to make a speech; the *Baywatch* girl did posturing and miming; and Chantelle, who we'd been told was a young star with a huge hit in Japan, was going to perform a number; I can't remember what Faria did, or Dennis Rodman, or Jodie Marsh.

Big Brother said that for every task set, the group would be either rewarded or else punished if one person stepped out of line or didn't do it properly and failed to achieve the necessary. Very quickly you realised that you had to do your best not just for yourself but for the group, otherwise food rations would be cut or cigarettes or alcohol would not be permitted. So it was a big responsibility. You had to forget your own embarrassment and niggles about not being able to do whatever tasks you were given.

I got some semblance of a costume together for Lady Macbeth and we all did our bit, and everybody was applauded, especially because everybody was doing what they were good at. It was a great icebreaker. I remember thinking how strange it was that Chantelle, if she was a lead singer, didn't know the lyrics of her own song and had to read them. Everyone else was most impressive.

Galloway would gather us together and say, 'This is us against the Big Brother team, brothers and sisters,' as the sort of leader. At first it was quite comforting, but it did start to pall a bit and I began to be suspicious when he said it was all for the good of the group. There were things about him that made me feel uncomfortable, though we got on well and we had a lot of interesting conversations together.

Pete Burns and I quickly came to blows. I made some comment like 'Do you regard yourself as a man, or as a woman?' and he blew his top. And I said, 'Well, I don't quite understand. If you don't want to be thought of as a woman, why do you dress as a woman? Why do you wear all that make-up and all those wigs and everything?'

So we got off on a bad footing, but he was absolutely compelling viewing and he had made all sorts of special deals with Big Brother because he occasionally commandeered the toilet for an hour at a time to put on his slap. You never saw him without his full make-up on.

At the end of the first day, when our suitcases arrived and we were unpacking, Pete Burns pulled out a huge shaggy fur coat – black and white – and he called it his gorilla coat, and I said, 'Pete, that's not a gorilla. There are no black and white gorillas. That's either a yak or even worse, a colobus monkey, which is an endangered species.' All hell broke loose. Big Brother must have expected this. They knew exactly what was in all our suitcases, and they knew I was a wildlife champion and a conservationist. At one point Big Brother confiscated the coat and had wildlife people come in to test it and see what it was. It turned out to be yak.

But the seeds of enmity between Pete Burns and myself were well and truly sown. Throughout the time I was in there I tried to understand him and I had lots of conversations with him about his plastic surgery procedures and he was very open about what had happened to him and his enormous, extraordinary mouth, which he claimed had been ruined through drugs and surgery and been reconstituted using human foreskins. He was very proud of that.

Some of the challenges were strange, some of them silly, some of them downright impossible. Pete Burns had to carry round a plant with him all day and keep talking to it. I was put into a room with a goldfish bowl and had to talk to this goldfish and find out its name and where it had come from. Faria had to be in a wheelbarrow all the time and be wheeled around the place.

And at one point Chantelle and Preston, who were already flirting with each other, were taken off to another room somewhere and we could see on the television screen that they were getting it on together. I became quite friendly with Maggot, the other young pop star, and Faria, who came across as a little bit flaky and shaky and insecure. I'm a bit of a mother hen, I like mothering and looking after people. I was feeling OK, apart from being very bored and realising quite quickly that just being yourself was not enough.

I didn't have a burning ambition to win but I didn't want to be the first person voted out. I wanted to be fair and I wanted to do whatever task I was given to the best of my ability so the group wouldn't be punished.

On more than one occasion, Pete Burns, in a fit of temper or whatever, just decided to be contrary and wouldn't do a task and then we were all punished. The first punishment was withdrawal of food. And there was one occasion when we had to choose between milk and toilet paper. And right towards the end of my stay, there were two days when there was *nothing* to eat and no tea and no coffee. At one point we made a meal out of potato peelings, covered in tomato ketchup and pepper and salt.

I'm not a person who gives in easily but there were several moments when I thought, 'This is just cruel.' I understood that it was for the amusement of the public outside but Big Brother was pushing people into really uncomfortable positions. I have with shame to admit that when the cigarettes ran out and we didn't have enough money to buy more because food and milk and basic staples were more important, Barrymore and I were on hands and knees outside scrabbling together for leftover stubs and rolling them in cigarette papers.

And when you take caffeine away from people, particularly people who are recovering alcoholics and slightly obsessive-compulsive, which Barrymore was, it's extraordinary what happens. I'm not a huge coffee drinker but I am a big tea drinker and when that is taken away and you have no food and nothing to do and tempers are worn and you are getting at each other's throats, horrible situations arise. Galloway and Pete Burns sometimes threw their weight around and that was painful to watch.

I wasn't going to allow myself to be destroyed in any way whatsoever. I decided very early that integrity and dignity were the two things I wanted to come out of the house with, and I was not going to be humiliated either by the Big Brother machine or by the people in there. Everybody seemed to know who I was, but that was more because of who I'd been married to. The younger ones certainly weren't aware of what I had done because *Rock Follies* was long before their time.

CHAPTER 22

HE WAS A CAT, I WAS HIS MISTRESS

Then came the famous moment when George Galloway and I were given an improvisation to do in the little room where I used to chant. It was very cramped and there was a small table and everything was bolted to the floor. You couldn't move the furniture. We were dressed in strange sort of orange prison uniforms and Galloway was told he was a cat and I was his mistress and for some reason he wasn't eating his food and I, as an animal lover, had to find out why he wasn't eating.

He really went into this improvisation wholeheartedly and I had no misgivings whatsoever. I was trying to act out this scenario as best as I could. I started stroking his head and he crawled towards me and put his head in my lap, and I was tickling his ears and saying, 'Poor little puddycat. What's the matter with you?' And he was meowing and purring and all the rest of it.

At the time we just thought we'd done it rather well and

congratulated each other. Only later, when I came out, did I see how it had been filmed, to make it look completely not what it was. It looked very strange and quite salacious. And one of the biggest shocks in the interview with Davina McCall afterwards were the headlines in all the papers with this compromising photograph of George Galloway's head in my crotch. It was even on the front of the *New York Times*. After thirty-five years in the business, playing many dozens of parts in everything from Shakespeare to *Morecambe and Wise*, not to mention *Rock Follies*, I sometimes get the horrible feeling this is what people remember me for. Galloway got most of the flak for it, but it was still a slightly uncomfortable situation for me. I can only thank God that it wasn't my head in his crotch.

That day or the next I got a chest infection or bronchitis or something. I had been smoking for England, I must admit, and I was really unwell, with a temperature, and I stayed one whole day in bed, then I got summoned into the diary room and hiding behind the diary room door was a doctor who examined me and listened to my chest and I wasn't allowed to tell anyone I had seen a doctor. I was prescribed antibiotics that Big Brother would have to dole out to me. Every time I had to take medication Big Brother would call me into the diary room.

They were very solicitous about my health and asked whether I wanted to leave and I said 'absolutely no way'. But

I spent about two days out of action, most of the time just lying down. And I have to say, the rest of the inmates were not terribly warm and caring about that. I wasn't allowed to tell them I was on antibiotics and really poorly. Maybe they thought it was all some sort of diva action.

Jodie Marsh, the glamour model, was the first person voted out. They were incredibly cruel to her. In fact, I took her under my wing a bit because I felt sorry for her. But everybody heaved a huge sigh of relief, because the one thing nobody wants is to be the first voted off. By now it was obvious that Chantelle and Preston were really into each other, and they were very friendly with me. She used to call me Mama Rula. At one point – I think this was before the real hunger days – Maggot was in tears. We cried a lot, with the exception of Pete Burns.

I never cried in public, only in the toilet or under my bedcover, but I did lose my cool a few times. When that happened I just removed myself from the situation because I knew I was liable to say things that would antagonise people I might be with for days to come.

Dennis Rodman really just wanted to get into women's knickers. I didn't have very much to do with him. He spent a lot of time in the gym pumping iron. He seemed to fancy Faria more than anybody, and the *Baywatch* girl, who may have known him from before.

I don't think he fancied me. No, I don't think anybody in there fancied me, although at the beginning it certainly seemed that Galloway and I were going to be good friends. But then, as I say, I found him a bit devious. I know he desperately wanted to win, as indeed did Michael Barrymore and Pete Burns. You would see two of them clubbing up together late at night. First it was Galloway and Barrymore but towards the end it was Galloway and Pete Burns, a most unlikely partnership.

We found out that poor Michael Barrymore had been allowed to bring sweets in. Every so often he would give us a jelly baby. And I know Pete Burns was given a different set of rules from everybody else because the Big Brother machine knew he was absolutely compulsive viewing, and in the little bits I watched afterwards, he was virtually in every single frame and he didn't disappoint.

There were moments when I felt incredibly homesick. Every single morning we were woken with either the dogs or this death knell tolling or a pop song that one of them had made famous – Pete Burns's 'You Spin Me Right Round', for instance – or somebody playing the violin horribly badly, and all incredibly loud, so you woke to a barrage of hideous sounds.

There were pedestals put up outside, numbered from one to eleven, and we had to decide amongst ourselves which of us was the most famous and organise ourselves in descending rank. You can imagine what happened. I think it was between Galloway and Barrymore as to who was the most famous – and then somebody, probably Galloway, said, 'You know, I think it might be Rula Lenska.' But I was put number three. I think in the end it was Barrymore, Galloway then me, then Pete Burns.

The two young boys wouldn't allow Chantelle to be last. If she'd been placed last in that line-up she would almost certainly have been voted out of the house but, instead, she remained a woman of mystery. By the time it was revealed that she wasn't a celebrity at all and just put into the house by the producers to pretend to be one, she had won the whole thing. Then she became very famous for a while.

I was in there for sixteen days. I was number five out. And just before I left there had been a horrid bullying session with the *Baywatch* girl. Pete Burns and George Galloway were incredibly cruel to her. I was told by Davina when I came out (whether this is true or not I don't know) that it was the sympathy vote between her and me for that week. Funnily enough, George Galloway was one of the first people to be nominated for voting out but he outlasted me and had quite a lot to do with me being thrown out.

There was one incident when Maggot got really upset, I'm not quite sure why. But I was comforting him and I remember saying, 'It's all right. We'll win this. We'll get through it. We'll be fine.' Not meaning that we'd win the competition but, you know, win over the odds or whatever. And when people were taken into another room and filmed and we could see what they were saying, Galloway said, 'I've heard her saying she's going to win this and she's lying if she says she doesn't want to win it.'

We would gather for the voting-out process, and Davina would say, 'Big Brother house, this is Davina. You are live on Channel 4; please do not swear', and we'd all be in the room where the furniture couldn't be moved and everybody would of course be dressed up to the nines, with the full make-up and jewellery just in case it was them who was going. And it took an awfully long time and it was incredibly nerve-racking. By the time I got out I was sort of longing to get out. Actually, no. Part of me was longing to get out but part of me was longing to say, 'I'll show you, Mr Galloway.'

There had been moments in the house which were enjoyable and very funny but there were moments which were terribly lonely and very frightening. And you had to resist wanting to let go, wanting to confide in somebody, wanting to cry or hide away in a corner, which of course you couldn't do. There was nowhere to hide and that took its toll. Not for long, but it did take its toll.

Being voted out is the most extraordinary sensation. It was a bit like coming out of prison except that you emerge into a barrage of flashing cameras and people screaming and shouting and you're all dressed up and smiling and putting on a great big act. Then you finally go into a quiet space for about ten minutes. My daughter and my agent and my sister were there and I just broke down.

I remember collapsing into the arms of my daughter, weeping and weeping and weeping and weeping, having held all of that in for such a long time. Then I went into this big circular space with Davina, who is absolutely lovely, and the first thing I see on these enormous screens right round this space are the photographs of George Galloway with his head in my crotch. There was talk at one point, and I'm not sure how serious it was, about the two of us doing a cat food commercial, which could have been incredibly lucrative.

Certainly from being someone I thought I admired he went down a good couple of notches. He's a fantastic speaker and a highly intelligent man, but there was this element of cruelty, his aggressiveness, that was not at all what I had expected. He has a huge ego. He likes marrying. What's he on – wife number four?

I was absolutely intent on watching every single programme after that, to see whether I was being talked about and how the dynamics were developing in the house, because by this time there was the Preston/Chantelle thing and the constant changing of the triangle of Barrymore, Galloway and Pete Burns.

I was offered the chance to see the psychiatrist again. I said no, I didn't need that. It took a good week to adjust after I got out and a funny thing – another echo of my prison days – I couldn't bear to have a door shut. I had to sleep with the bedroom door open. But above all there was the euphoria of actually having weathered it and survived.

I think I came out of it with my dignity intact, which is important. And then there was the joy of being able to write a cheque for £20,000 to the David Sheldrick Wildlife Trust – some of it paid for a little Suzuki Jeep with my name on it running around Kenya; £10,000 to the Tibetan Midwifery Training School – that sort of money can make an enormous amount of difference in places like that; £3,000 went to the Born Free Foundation and their work with tigers in Siberia; £8,000 for gorillas in Cameroon; £3,000 to Animals Asia to help rescue bears from the horrifically cruel farms where their bile is extracted for use in Chinese medicine. It made up for moments of hell in there. It was marvellous, being able to give that amount away, because I'll never be able to do it again in my life.

As part of the *Big Brother* contract I had to do a newspaper interview and it happened to be with a journalist I knew – albeit not very well – called Lester Middlehurst. It was a very positive article with a nice photograph, and he briefly mentioned my youthful Sardinian escapade when I was working in a nightclub and got sent to jail.

I was at home just getting ready to leave for the theatre – I was on tour in Stephen Daldry's brilliant production of J. B. Priestley's *An Inspector Calls* – and the phone rang and this vaguely recognisable foreign voice says, 'Ciao, principessa.' I said, 'Who are you?' And he said, in Italian, 'You don't recognise my voice? It's the great love of your life.'

So I thought, 'I don't believe this!' And it was Gianni, my lover from the Sardinia days, and I said, 'My God! How extraordinary to hear from you. Where are you?' And he said, 'I'm in England and I would really love to see you.'

I hadn't had any contact with him for thirty-five years. And, being on my own and having some fond memories, I agreed to meet up with him.

So we had lunch. He was still incredibly sexy and swarthy and Italian and very warm and caring and we did a lot of catching up. We talked about various other people who'd been around when we'd had the prison escapade. He asked me whether I was working at the moment. And I said, 'Yes, I'm in a play at a theatre not too far from home in High Wycombe.' And he said, 'Oh I would love to see it,' and I said, 'Well, it's a wordy play, I don't think you'll understand very much of it.' And he said, 'Nevertheless, nevertheless, I'd love to see you.'

I agreed that the following day I would pick him up and take him down for the show. And we drove down, and because I needed an hour or more to get myself ready, he went walkabout. Then he watched the show and came back to my dressing room afterwards. As we were leaving the theatre there were paparazzi at the stage door and others who jumped out from behind the hedges. Even more extraordinarily, he didn't seem particularly fazed by it.

We got into the car and I said, 'I wonder what that was all about.' And we talked a little bit about the play and of course he hadn't understood it. And as we're nearing London, I said to him, 'Where do you want me to drop you off?' and he said 'Can't I stay at yours?' And my initial reaction, knowing what he was like, was, 'Er, no. I don't think that's a very good idea.' He said, 'Please, please, there's still so much catching up to do.' So finally I agreed, as long as there's no funny business and he ended up sleeping in the spare room upstairs. I got up in the morning fairly early because I had a matinée and he was already up and looking distinctly worried and nervous about something. I took him to the train station and he said he'd be in touch again before he left to go back to Italy. And I never really found out what he had come over here for. He mentioned something about some business deal.

I was driving down to High Wycombe for the matinée when I got a phone call from Lester Middlehurst and he said, 'Look, this may be absolutely nothing, but I thought as we know each other, I'd pass it by you just to make sure. Do you know somebody called Gianni Bussu?' And I said, 'Yes. How extraordinary, I was with him yesterday.' And Lester said, 'He's just been into the office and apparently he's made a deal with one of the tabloids for rather a lot of money, claiming that he's been having an ongoing relationship with you all through your marriage to Dennis.'

'What? Absolute rubbish,' I told him. Lester said, 'He claims he has paper evidence.' To which I said, 'Well, the only correspondence I had with him was in prison and immediately after prison for a year or so and those documents have dates on, unless he doctored them in some sort of way.' And Lester, very sweetly, said, 'Look, if there is no truth in this matter then I'll somehow be able to scotch the story.'

It turned out that a girlfriend of my sister Anna had a husband who was a great friend of Gianni's. He had seen the article in the paper, seen the snippet about the Sardinian prison and sent it to him and said, 'Here's an opportunity to make a tidy sum of money.' Anyway, Lester, bless him, managed to kill the story. I found it really hard to believe that someone with whom I'd had a genuine love affair, and shared a prison ordeal, could do the dirty like that. I tried to track him down but failed until a couple of years later when I did manage to get in touch, and I asked him, 'How could you think of doing something like that?' And he said, 'Oh, I was going to share the money with you.'

Needless to say, we have never spoken again.

With Peter Sellers in Soft Beds, Hard Battles,
1974 – fully clothed this time!

CHAPTER 23

IN BED WITH PETER SELLERS...

When I was twenty-six I had a double debut – in film and in bed. I have rarely been seen by the public in either since. My bedmate was Peter Sellers playing a British double agent. At other times in *Soft Beds, Hard Battles* he was Hitler, Charles de Gaulle and the Emperor of Japan, amongst others. I was one of seven scantily clad girls in a brothel run by Lila Kedrova – I'd loved her in *Zorba the Greek*, one of my favourites. In bed with me Mr Sellers was a perfect gentleman. Though we were both naked he told me there was nothing to worry about, there would be a sheet between us. Later, when he had to pin a Croix de Guerre on my lapel he dropped it down my cleavage. He seemed nervous, his mind clearly on other things; he was in the middle of an affair with Liza Minnelli.

Though we ladies were required on set dressed and ready for action at 7.30 a.m. he sometimes didn't turn up till noon, but none of us ever complained. I was excited just to be in his presence. He was a genius, hilarious but also profoundly insecure. After an absolutely side-splitting scene where he played Hitler he came up to me and to my amazement asked, 'Was I really funny? Did you believe what I was trying to be?'

The film, made by the Boulting brothers, was not a great success. It wasn't Sellers's finest moment, nor mine, but it was still a fantastic thrill. Because he had to wear so many facial prosthetics there was a life-size plaster cast of his head. I begged to keep it and I have it to this day.

The following year I narrowly avoided a bed scene of a rather different kind. I was a sort of handmaiden to the courtesan Lola Montez in *Royal Flash*, Richard Lester's Flashman film. Malcolm McDowell was Flashman. One evening the whole cast was eating and drinking good champagne in our rather fancy hotel when Oliver Reed, one of the stars of the film, strode in with a couple of very commanding-looking body-guards. He was already very well oiled. He looked round the room. Almost everybody was with their other halves. Then he saw me. 'Who are you with?' he asked. 'I'm by myself,' I said. 'Not for tonight you're not. Your luck has changed. Be outside my suite at midnight,' he said in a disturbingly authoritative voice. Perhaps because he was playing Otto von Bismarck and we were in Germany it felt like an order from on high, but really it was probably just normal business for Oliver Reed.

A little while later I excused myself, ran to my room and locked myself in. Just after midnight there was knock at the door. It was one of his minders. 'Mr Reed is waiting.' I just sat there in the dark with my heart pounding until I was sure he had gone. Battle was not joined.

A far more ghastly experience was in *Queen Kong*, a low-budget item and surely a contender for the worst film ever made. The ape was a woman and Robin Askwith was her love interest. I played a character called Luce Habit – by now you can probably imagine just how bad it was. I was in charge of a boat with a crew of beautiful girls sailing the seven seas, which were mostly the lake at Pinewood. The production ran out of money and I don't think I ever got paid. Happily, it was hardly seen here though it did become a massive cult in Japan, which is no consolation.

❧

When you are acting in the open air unpredictable things happen. If it's *A Midsummer Night's Dream* and the fairies are all on stage, out of nowhere will come a gust of wind and all the costumes float up in the air. And if it's Regent's Park and you're so near to the zoo, you might hear a lion roar or a bird screech at the very moment when you're talking about an animal – almost as if they'd been scripted.

I was Titania, queen of the fairies in Ian Talbot's production of the *Dream* in Regent's Park in 1978. One evening I was asleep in the bower – you have to lie on stage for quite a long time – and a squirrel came out of nowhere and jumped up on to my hip.

A squirrel would never normally come near a person, not unless you've got something to eat – and it just sat there for about two minutes. It was as if he was saying to me, 'Out of this wood do not desire to go / Thou shalt remain here, whether thou wilt or no,' which would have been a damn cheek. Those were my lines – or maybe he was just being obedient.

In 1981 I was offered my first panto – starring Bernard Bresslaw as Abanazar, Les Dawson as Widow Twankey, Christopher Timothy as Wishy-Washy and me as Aladdin. Arthur Askey did a tiny little spot in the show too. Wonderful! A stellar cast, in Richmond, just down the road from home, and I had the most glamorous principal boy's role of them all.

We rehearsed in a room off the Fulham Road and I remember falling under Les's spell the first time I met him. He was unbelievably funny, but there was a touching vulnerability about him and we became good friends fairly quickly. At the time, his wife was very ill with cancer. Les lived in Lytham St Annes and he was commuting, being driven up and down – 240 miles each way – on almost a daily basis during rehearsals and when we were performing.

It was a very tough time for him but he was wonderful with the children in the panto – this rotund father figure, with a great sense of humour and a twinkle in his eye. Rehearsing with him was incredibly funny because he never stuck to the script and with him it didn't matter. You never felt you were skating on thin ice, you always knew he was going to be able to rescue you if anything happened.

In *Aladdin* there's the traditional slosh scene with Widow Twankey in the launderette with foam and water flying all over the stage. I know from other pantos I've done since how incredibly careful they are, laying tarpaulins so that this slippery stuff doesn't go everywhere. But with Les that would be impossible. He didn't take any notice of where the suds ended up and he did it differently every time. In the next scene Bernard Bresslaw, who was a marvellously evil Abanazar and absolutely massive, had to push me into a cave, which was a front cloth, while they cleared up the mess behind it. It was all supposed to be very organised and controlled but there was Fairy Liquid and foam all over the place.

At the dress rehearsal Bernard and I both fell head over heels and he landed on top of me and if you remember Bernard Bresslaw you will know that's no small thing. They had no option but to cut out some of the water chucking and some of the other custard-pie stuff so everyone could get through the evening in one piece.

Richmond Theatre had tiny, tiny dressing rooms backstage and Les, or King Bumbly as he used to call himself, was in the next-door dressing room to me and he used to drink virtually a bottle of Scotch before the show, but you would never know it. Even though he was living through a very trying and traumatic time at home, he was always firing on all cylinders and had time for everybody.

It wasn't long since I had first met Dennis and we had started our relationship. Dennis and I would get together occasionally between shows. And I used to talk to Les at length about the relationship. Les told me he knew Dennis quite well because they'd seen each other at various football and cricket testimonials and charity events.

He told me, 'Be careful with Dennis, because he likes being surrounded by women and he is a flirt and I don't want you to get hurt.' I very clearly remember him saying that. And Les and I used to go out in the evening to local pubs where Dennis and one or two of his entourage would occasionally join us. So Les was a little bit like a chaperone, and just a delight.

In another scene Princess Scheherazade was singing in her cherry blossom garden and everything was pink and twinkly and beautiful and gorgeous and there was a white picket fence at the back of the stage and I was waiting in the wings for my next entrance, when suddenly Les strides across the stage – hidden from the audience from the waist down – stark naked, but still with his Widow Twankey wig on, gurning. We were absolutely falling over ourselves with laughter. And every time I came on stage – and he came up to about my armpit – he used to say, 'Oh, come here my son, come here!' It was really hard to keep a straight face with him, impossible actually.

Traditionally, at the end of every panto, usually during

the last matinée, people play jokes on each other, so I knew something ridiculous was afoot. I started my big number in the show with some foreboding; it was the song 'Somewhere' from the musical *West Side Story*. I suspected something fishy because Les was likely to be on the case. I was centre stage, on my own, ready to sing my heart out to the audience, but as I started the whole audience burst out laughing – I mean gales of laughter – and I couldn't understand why. But they all seemed to be pointing upwards. So I look up and there are hundreds of paper fish – plaice – dropped in from the flies, all bobbing along to me singing 'There's a place for us'.

✤

I didn't always need the services of a great comedian like Les Dawson to make me look like an idiot on stage. Sometimes I could do it all by myself. When I was very young, I was working in rep at Westcliff-on-Sea. It was in the days when I was with Pavlik, my Russian boyfriend, who had given me a London taxi, and that effectively made me the company chauffeur. I was always ferrying people around. Actually, there was plenty to deal with without that. In rep you're doing one play in the evening, rehearsing another one during the day and possibly thinking about a third play that's coming next. And on top of that you may have to learn how to roller skate.

I was playing Miss 1940 in Peter Nichols's *Forget-Me-Not*

Lane. I wore a Union Jack headdress and I had to perform on Union Jack roller skates. Anyway, I'd been practising my roller skating on the promenade and I was feeling quite good about it. Of course we'd had no time to rehearse in the theatre.

There was a crucial difference between the prom and the stage. Westcliff prom is flat, the stage was raked – not that anyone had told me. For my first entrance a door swung open, the music had started to play, I was supposed to march down on my roller skates to the front of the stage, smartly swivel, turn and go back upstage. I should be so lucky. I came marching down the stage, couldn't stop myself, fell straight into the orchestra pit and twisted my ankle quite badly, but still managed somehow to go on. I haven't acted on roller skates again and don't expect to called up for *Starlight Express* any time soon.

In the late 1980s I played Elvira in Noël Coward's *Blithe Spirit*. The production started life at the Lyric Theatre in Hammersmith and then we did a long tour with it. As befits the ghost of a woman who's been dead seven years, I was extremely pale, an effect achieved by covering me in glittery white make-up. I looked the part but I was leaving white handprints all over the place. The piano, for instance, was covered with them. Something had to be done. I decided hairspray was the answer. Not my best idea. I covered myself in it after I'd put on the white glittery make-up. I didn't leave handprints any more, but I stuck to everything.

Peggy Mount was playing the spiritualist Madame Arcati, who conjured me up. She was absolutely adorable, funny and wonderful in the part, but every now and again she would break wind on stage, which used to reduce the whole cast into uncontrollable fits of giggles. It happened at moments of high dudgeon or laughter and usually she wasn't aware she'd done it but something would gently sort of become not so much heard as smelt. It could have been a ghostly ether wafted in from 'the other side' but I doubt it.

❦

At just the time Dennis had run off to Australia and left me, I was asked whether I would be interested in doing *A Little Night Music* at the Theatre Royal, Plymouth, playing the part of Desiree and of course getting to sing 'Send in the Clowns', one of my all-time favourite Stephen Sondheim songs. To play Desiree and sing that song would be a huge buzz. But, even better, Glynis Johns, the original Desiree, was cast as my mother. Stephen Sondheim wrote the song specially for her, it wasn't in the original book, and the joy of it is you don't have to be a singer. In fact it helps if you have a gravelly voice. That's the song for me!

There were to be three weeks' rehearsal and a month's run so obviously I was going to be staying down in Plymouth. On the first day of rehearsal in walked Glynis Johns, looking absolutely gorgeous with this blonde hair, divine scent, all dressed in pink – very glossy and dewy-eyed; she read absolutely beautifully and then left the read-through. Rehearsals started the following day but no Glynis Johns. No Glynis Johns the next day, nor the day after that. And each time the director would come up with some different excuse – she had an infection, or her ingrown toenail was giving her a problem, or she had a stomach upset.

By the end of the week, still no Glynis Johns; halfway through the second week, still no Glynis Johns. We were all getting really worried about this but the director said, 'Don't worry, she's played it a million times before, she'll be fine. Even if she only comes in three days beforehand, she'll be absolutely fine.' Fine for her, but what about the rest of us? It was a very difficult set, because there a huge gap in the middle of the stage where the mini orchestra was.

They had paid a lot for Miss Johns and she was put up in the best suite in the biggest hotel in Plymouth. With the permission of the director I decided to go and visit her after rehearsals towards the end of the second week. I was shown up to this very elegant suite and there she was, in her bed, with a fluffy pink wrap and perfumed pink lip gloss – the whole room smelt absolutely divine. I remember being struck by how many bottles of Perrier water were dotted around, on every available surface.

Anyway, for whatever reason, she never turned up. This wonderful women called Eileen Page took the part over with four days to go. Glynis gave me a painted clown as a first-night present. I still take it with me when I'm working and it has pride of place on my dressing table. But it was a big disappointment not being able to work with her.

Then, when I was two weeks into the show, I got a phone call from a very drunk Mr Waterman, from Australia, at three o'clock in the morning, saying, 'Waterman here, I want to come home.' So he came and I think he saw the final performance.

Dennis always said I took silly risks with animals and he was probably right. I was playing the part of a ringmaster in *Casualty* and because of my love for and stupidity about animals I nearly became just that – a casualty. The circus we were filming with had elephants and big cats and I am against the idea of animals in circuses. I asked not to be photographed with them and the director kindly agreed. But naturally I wanted to make their acquaintance so I asked the keeper if I could give buns and sandwiches to the elephants. He said, 'Certainly, but don't go into their tent on your own.' But, of course, I did.

They had warned me that when an elephant stretches its trunk it can always reach another foot further if it really wants to. So I went in and gave a treat to each of the elephants but I was one treat short. As I was leaving, the elephant who had missed out reached out and lashed out, giving me a nasty smack on the backside and sending me flying. I felt like a fool but it could have been a whole lot worse.

※

In 2004 I was asked if I would be interested in doing *The Vagina Monologues*. I'd heard about it, of course, but I hadn't seen it, so I was invited to go and watch the current cast at the Arts Theatre near Leicester Square. Siân Phillips was in it. I remember thinking how incredibly brave the women were. I was also very touched by the content, knowing that they were all true stories. It really has got everything – it's very funny, it's extremely moving, very touching and just a strange and completely different theatrical experience. So I said, 'Yes, I would love to do it.'

I went to meet the director Irina Brown, a Russian lady, a couple of times. Then there was one meeting with the other girls on the day before my first performance. The director decides which of the threesome gets which monologues and you don't immediately see the other monologues you're not doing. The most frightening one I was given ended with the thirteen fake orgasms. It's the end of the show and in a way the star piece.

I'd been acting for well over three decades by then but I've never been so scared, both because of the content and because I knew from seeing the show how loved it was by the audience, which was predominantly female. On that occasion I didn't have to do the C-word monologue, but I remember the first time that I heard it, I blushed absolutely crimson. I knew that the girl doing that monologue had to get the audience to chant the C-word and you think, this is never going to happen – but it does, without fail, wherever you are.

It doesn't matter how old, or how big, the audience is, they do it, even the most unexpected people, including my dear stepmother, who came to see the show at the age of about eighty-two. She was one of the few elderly relatives who did see it. I told some of the others who would have disapproved that I was doing *The 'Angina' Monologues*. My daughter knew the script inside out because she'd listened to my lines. In fact, she'd been very supportive because I thought I'd probably better ask her before I agreed to do it, and she said, 'Absolutely, go ahead and do it, Mum.'

She came to my first night but apparently she couldn't listen to her mum saying those words on stage and spent the whole show hiding underneath her seat with her hands clapped over her ears.

I did it for a month at the Arts Theatre then I did three or four separate tours with different mixtures of women all over the country. Probably the most memorable, apart from my initial performances with Jenny Jules and Tilly Blackwood, were three weeks on the road with Miriam Margolyes and Jenny Eclair. I went on tour with several casts and we always had a wonderful time. The show sold out everywhere we went and the reaction from the audience was unbelievable, because it's very cathartic and very much about empowering your femininity.

I got the most amazing letters from people who had been abused, thanking us all for having helped them come to terms with it, and some from women who hadn't discovered their sexuality until much later in life. It was great fun to do and you actually felt you were doing good, helping some people with very difficult situations as well as raising a lot of money for abused women all over the world. I think it was an important show.

Then I did a musical called *Hot Flush*, which was about four women going through the menopause. We had two fabulous singers, Sheila Ferguson from The Three Degrees and Marti Webb – and me, who was by no means a singer. Sam Kane was the one and only man. He played about twenty-five different characters. Again, the audiences were females en masse; again, it was very successful. There was a live band on stage with us, so if you made a mistake and you forgot your lines or something happened, you had to get yourself out of it, which is hard enough when it's speaking – when it's singing it's really difficult, because if there's a backing track they can't stop it.

My first number was 'What Has She Got That I Haven't?' and I'm coming down a staircase in very high heels singing 'What has she got that I haven't? I've got the brains she hasn't...' and I got my heel caught, forgot my lines and the music carried on playing, so I got the shoe back on, finally, strutted across the stage and at the end of the number, I said, 'That was a real menopausal moment,' and I got a huge round of applause, so the audience was on my side from the beginning.

❀

A couple of years later I was in *Calendar Girls*, the Yorkshire Women's Institute nude calendar story which had already been a successful film before it was made into a play that toured and toured. I was in the fourth version, so it had already been all over the country and was going back to the same theatres time and time again and selling out absolutely everywhere, to largely female audiences.

We did enormous venues like Blackpool Opera House,

which was a 3,000-seater. Very raucous. The set was absolutely minimal and the whole show was short scenes, seamlessly running together, very often without the curtain coming down.

There were seven women in the play. Most of the time it was a very happy company. I was the only new person on that tour. All the others had done it at least twice before. Lynda Bellingham had been in it from the beginning, so this was number five for her. The big difficulty for me at first, coming in to a show that had already been done many times before, was that I didn't have the opportunity to actually make it my own from the beginning. It was a bit dead men's, or dead women's, shoes. But then as the play runs, you do find moments which you make your own.

The climax of the show, of course, is the photographic session where all the women are in various stages of undress. But it was very subtly done and you honestly don't see anything. Occasionally a bit of masking would slip, and in my case I was the first person to strip my top off and I had a pyramid of cakes topped with two Chelsea Buns at sort of breast level. Some of the stages we worked on were very steeply raked and this cake pyramid was on a trolley with wheels. So if the wheels didn't get properly jammed or they forgot to put the lock on, I would be standing behind a pyramid of cakes as it was gently rolling away, and I couldn't hold onto that because I had to hold onto my breasts. It took some courage to do it the first time. It was almost as frightening as *The Vagina Monologues*.

❧

You can't spend years working in the theatre without experiencing some painful moments, falling on your face metaphorically and sometimes literally. During the *Calendar Girls* tour I fell over a pile of cables which hadn't been properly covered with masking tape and ripped the rotator cuff on my right shoulder, which unfortunately is going to be with me for the rest of my life, but I didn't miss a performance.

I have had to drop out once or twice in pantomime when I've lost my voice, but only once or twice. You have to do so much shrieking and shouting to be heard above the kids when you're playing the baddie, even though there are microphones. I've done every pantomime there is to be done. I've played all the principal boys, all the fairy godmothers and the Wicked Queen in *Snow White* three times. I don't take panto lightly. It's very hard work – two shows, sometimes three shows a day and it's a big responsibility because it's most young children's first experience of the theatre.

I think my favourite was *Robinson Crusoe*, with Dennis playing my brother and Jan Leeming playing the figurehead on the prow of the ship – we had a wonderful time. And of the female roles, the Wicked Queen in *Snow White* is the greatest fun to do. I did that three times with John Inman and Lionel Blair. I enjoy panto but it really does take it out of you.

I had done a television series – *Take a Letter, Mr Jones* – with

John Inman and we got on incredibly well. And we did pantos at Wimbledon and Woking together. There was one particular routine where John Inman dresses up as the Wicked Queen, and of course we couldn't have been more different in size and shape and everything else. And it's this complete mirror reflection, where he's mirroring me and I keep trying to catch him out and finally I do – and it's quite a long, clever routine and he was always very exact. A wonderful dancer and very prim and proper and his make-up was always absolutely perfect, a bit of a contrast with Les Dawson – his lipstick would always be halfway up his nose.

My most cherished theatre part in recent years came in *84 Charing Cross Road*, based on a true story about an older American woman who is an avid book collector and makes contact with a bookshop, Marks & Co in Charing Cross Road, and this twenty-year relationship begins to evolve from the letters that pass between her and the bookseller Frank Doel. They never actually meet but it is like a love story through books and communications about books. She is on her own in a garret in New York. Bill Gaunt, who's a terrific actor, played the man.

It was an absolutely wonderful role for me, a very well-written play and a beautiful production. It was a huge part and she's supposed to be fairly dowdy, rather dykey, and it was a great opportunity to get away from how people think of me physically. I wore a short, very dark wig and frumpy, unfitting, unattractive clothes.

I played Annie Wilkes in *Misery*, the part Kathy Bates plays in the film. I cut all my hair off and I didn't even wear a wig; no make-up or padding. My daughter used to lock her bedroom door because she was so scared of me.

I thought that because I was so unrecognisable it would alter the way people see me – it certainly worked with my daughter. But casting people don't seem to have a lot of imagination. When you're younger, before you have any sort of profile, you try to go for the interview or audition looking and dressing in the way that you might see the character. Obviously I'm not going to auditions now with no make-up or my hair under a net. You expect people to think that if you're going up for that part you are willing to look however that part needs you to look.

In 2005 I landed a small role in a film called *Gypo*. I was cast as a plain older Romanian refugee with no make-up and it was heartening to see how many people who saw it were incredibly complimentary. I've always wanted more opportunity to play away from the glamour image. Sadly it doesn't happen very often.

Some of my happiest working times have been when I have been heard but not seen. It must be about thirty-five years since I did my first talking book and they have given me a lot of pleasure.

At first the books I was given mostly involved Eastern European characters, convoluted spy stories generally taking place in the Baltic countries. But eventually I graduated and was allowed to record stories involving Brits. To this day I do six or eight a year and it has remained a delight.

Talking into a microphone for eight hours daily is not an easy thing to do, but it is exciting and a challenge to capture an audience with just your voice. And you don't have to worry about what you look like.

These days I mostly do it in Bath, which is a pleasure in itself. I am always put up at a really good hotel, either the Bath Spa or the Royal Crescent, so it is a mini holiday, particularly the Bath Spa, which lives up to its name in the sauna, massage and pampering department. The whole gig is like belonging to a charming little club. The studios are cosy and over the years I have got to know nearly all the producers and have met many fascinating, brilliant and amusing actors in the reading game, amongst others Timothy West, Prunella Scales, Derek Jacobi, David Tennant, Patrick Stewart, Christopher Timothy, Claire Higgins and Clarissa Dickson Wright. Clarissa Dickson Wright isn't an actor, of course, but she's a very good act. So more often than not there are hilarious lunches to be had on working days when we put down our books and eat.

I recall one occasion, a very hot and sultry day, before air conditioning was installed in the studios, sitting in my little box no bigger than a toilet, facing a large window, on the other side of which sat my producer, Mellie Buse. It was late afternoon, when a sort of tiredness and word-blindness tends to set in and it was a long, over-descriptive, complicated spy story and we were both fighting drooping eyes and sleepiness.

'Chapter 16,' I read. 'The streets of Djibouti were overflowing with Arab seamen.' On the page it's just an ordinary sentence but read out loud it's a hysterical schoolgirl joke. And both of us responded like schoolgirls. My producer, who until that time had been dozing off, suddenly erupted in hoots of laughter and almost fell off her chair, and once I realised what I'd said it became impossible. We probably had fifteen takes before I was able to get the line out without a stifled giggle.

The other thing that frequently happens when reading aloud for long periods is that your tummy starts making some very strange noises because of the amount of air and saliva one swallows. I remember Mellie telling me that they had recorded a selection of these bodily noises from many different artists. I've always been extremely careful about what I order for my lunch on reading days.

Recently I had a Fay Weldon book to record, basically a series of monologues by various women characters, each one with a different regional accent. As I have always known, since drama school and before, regional accents aren't my strong point. Even when I was in *Coronation Street* my voice didn't move north of Watford. I could probably manage a vaguely generic cockney or Scottish if pushed hard. On this occasion one of the monologues had to be in Geordie. Try as I might, I found it impossible. Finally my producer, my very dear friend Kate, had to resort to giving me line-by-line readings which I would have to phonetically copy, a hysterical afternoon probably still not for Newcastle ears.

Recorded books have made useful presents for elderly Polish relatives who are no longer able to read so easily. They're my perfect audience. Not only do they love me, they couldn't tell a Brummie from a Scouser.

CHAPTER 24

DOING MY BIT FOR CHARITY

It is a cliché for people like me to say that being able to work for charities I care about is a privilege, but I'll say it and I mean it. Visiting displaced persons' camps in Hungary with and for the Red Cross brought home cruel realities in a way that reading or watching programmes about it never can, though for me it was not so remote – it reminded me of my mother's own experience during the Second World War, which was even worse.

Children in Crisis (CiC) is a charity that works all over the world to help chronically ill and deprived little ones, but it started much smaller than that. Originally called Angels, it was set up by my family and other members of the Polish community and dealt solely with Poland. Now with Sarah, Duchess of York as its patron it has really spread its wings. Part of the charity money I got for appearing on *Big Brother* went towards building a training scheme for midwives in Tibet, a project instigated by my friendship with the Buddhist priest Lama Norbu, whom I introduced to CiC.

But in 1992 it was to Poland that the Duchess, my sister Anna and I travelled to open a respite home for chronically ill children in Upper Silesia. The trip to Babia Góra was the joyous culmination of many years of fundraising. The home was terrific and there was a huge ceremonial opening with music and dancing and we had a wonderful time with the Duchess, both in our official capacities and when we were relaxing.

On our last night in Krakow we were having a celebratory dinner in one of the grand restaurants off the town square, which is dominated on one side by the Mariacki church. Although officially a church it has the dimensions of a cathedral and has an enchanting legend attached to it.

In the thirteenth century, on the same spot, there was a lookout tower used to warn the inhabitants of attacks by the Tartars. When such an attack was imminent a trumpeter would sound the alarm north, south, east and west. According to legend, during the haunting sound of the warning the trumpeter got shot through the throat by a Tartar arrow. To this day – four times a day, on the hour – the same tune is played live from the church tower and it breaks off on the note where the trumpeter was killed.

That evening just before midnight I decided that I had to take the Duchess out into the square to witness it. So, without thinking, I grabbed her hand and without explaining anything I dashed out with her to listen to the *hejnal*, which is the name for the tune in Polish. Just as the trumpeter was sounding for the third time to the east a couple of waiters rushed out after us, obviously under the impression we were trying to leave without paying the bill. 'REDHEADS CAUGHT RED-HANDED', the headlines would have read.

❧

There are five animal and conservation charities that have been very close to my heart for decades: the Born Free Foundation, the Environmental Investigation Agency, the David Shepherd Wildlife Foundation, Animals Asia and the David Sheldrick Wildlife Trust.

Three of these are led by remarkable women whom I consider dear friends. Virginia McKenna, so dedicated and determined, is of course titular head of the Born Free Foundation; as head of Animals Asia, Jill Robinson is responsible for saving the horrendously maltreated bears incarcerated in the ghastly Chinese bear bile farms; and then there's the wonderful Daphne Sheldrick – I visit her every time I go to Africa.

I first came across Daphne about twenty-five years ago when I narrated her life story for a programme in the BBC *Survival* series called 'The Orphans of Tsavo'. I was excited and pleased to be able to show her work to a wider public.

Some time later I was in Kenya again – my third visit to Daphne – to make a programme about the brilliant wildlife artist Gary Hodges. It was a particular pleasure because not only is he a marvellous practitioner, he is also a great friend and, since most of the filming was at Daphne Sheldrick's elephant orphanages, I was able again to spread the word. I remember those eleven days as filled with joy.

I was able to talk at length to this lady who really has given her whole life to returning abandoned, injured and orphaned elephants to the wild, and see how one woman's determination and the love and dedication of those who work with her can make a real difference. Of course, being passionate about elephants in particular, to be surrounded by them was pure magic!

In the nursery part of the orphanage there were six babies all under one year old, still being fed on demand, and with their keepers twenty-four hours a day. Vulnerable and traumatised (and one of them badly injured), the elephants spend peaceful days being gently cared for as their mental and physical strength is restored. We were told many times 'an elephant will only thrive when it is happy'. We also learnt from Daphne about all the other environmental projects she has instigated, ranging from anti-poaching patrols in Tsavo to educational programmes in Nairobi.

In Tsavo East National Park, which is home to Kenya's largest population of wild elephants, the young orphans who are no longer milk-dependent learn to be wild elephants. When we visited there were twenty-three of them, ranging from two to eight years old. It was a filming, photography and personal paradise! Gary and I spent our days in the thick of these intelligent, comical, gentle pachyderms.

We got some wonderful footage and there were many hilarious moments. Trying to conduct a serious interview surrounded by inquisitive trunks and flapping ears was no easy task but hugely enjoyable and very funny. Daphne's organisation (www.sheldrickwildlifetrust.org) has a 'foster an elephant' scheme. For only £50 a year you can become a foster parent. You will get monthly keeper reports and photos. It makes a wonderful present for a child, adult or group, and it really makes a difference. Giving money directly to the source and putting an elephant back into the wild again: all this is just a simple click away.

❧

I am not deaf – far from it – but I have problems in that area. Thanks to good hearing aids and a wonderful audiologist, Milanka Drenovak, who has stuck with me through thick and thin, it doesn't cause me too great difficulty personally or professionally.

Unfortunately, hearing loss carries a stigma. If you wear glasses or contact lenses, people understand it and only a fool would make silly comments, but jokes are always made about being 'mutton' (Mutt and Jeff is cockney rhyming slang for deaf, hence mutton). People don't appreciate what losing your hearing means. If someone had asked me years ago, 'What's worse, losing a lot of your sight or most of your hearing?' I would have immediately said sight; but it's frightening how alienating and frustrating it is when you have hearing loss, even with top-of-the-range hearing aids – they don't replicate what good ears hear.

People were sometimes calling me arrogant, because I wasn't replying to questions, and I found that I was staying away from social occasions. I can hear in a room full of people, but it's a struggle and sometimes I have problems in big rehearsal rooms that have a lot of echo. Going to the theatre sometimes is a problem.

Specsavers were doing this big hearing campaign and they asked me to front it, which of course meant I had to come clean. I thought, 'Yes, this is a good opportunity,' and in fact it took a huge weight off my mind to admit to it. The acting business is cut-throat. If you have failings or difficulties in certain areas, they can be used against you. I can function perfectly well in most situations, but it's much easier if people know. So I discussed it for a long time with my agent and other members of my family and I think in the end it was a good thing to do. I'm interested in making it easier for a lot of people who don't have the opportunities I've had to get really good help from audiology specialists.

We all know about guide dogs for the blind; far less well known are hearing dogs. I had a wonderful day at the centre in Buckinghamshire where they are taught to alert their owners by touch, and even had a little King Charles pup named after me. It was touching to see how much these dogs had changed the lives of the profoundly deaf people I met there and given them so much more independence than they would have enjoyed otherwise.

There was a particular gentleman I remember who developed the whole idea of subtitles, not just for the news, but for films and wildlife programmes and everything else. I thought I was in a good position to try and ease the stigma surrounding deafness, by writing articles and talking to people and saying that it's not the end of life. It's a difficult hurdle to get over but it helps if you admit it. If I have been helpful in educating people about it, I'm delighted.

'Betrayed by the tranny and the granny': Sue Nicholls as Audrey and me as Claudia in Coronation Street, *with Andrew Hall as Marc Selby in the background, 2011.*

CHAPTER 25

'WHAT, ME, IN *CORRIE*?'

After *Big Brother*, my agent and I decided we'd try and keep away from theatre work and touring shows and really look for something interesting in television. I had been asked before whether I wanted to go on *Emmerdale* and for some reason I chose not to. I had done a 'bubble' in *EastEnders* quite a few years back (a 'bubble' means it wasn't filmed in Albert Square – this was all on location in Spain, following a wonderful storyline over two episodes).

I never imagined there was really anything for me in the traditional English soaps, nothing substantial anyway. I just didn't see where I would fit in. I was hardly a candidate for *Coronation Street*, was I? I was thinking more about drama and hoping for a role in a good play or, even better, a three-parter.

I remember at the time I was chanting quite hard for something high profile that would pay decent money and this just proves how Buddhist chanting can work. Very often it has the sort of results you're hoping for but those results come to you from a completely different direction.

When my agent first rang me up and said, 'Look, they want to see you for about six or seven episodes of *Coronation Street*,' I said, 'Me, in *Coronation Street*? You've got to be joking. I can't do a northern accent and even if I could, it doesn't sit well on my sort of voice and it's hard to imagine me in the Rovers Return.'

I had never been a dedicated *Corrie* fan. I dipped in and out of it from time to time. My agent said, 'Listen, it's the longest-running and most popular of all the English soaps. I really do think you ought to go and meet them.' So I said OK and they sent me the first script to look at. I was Claudia Colby, an old friend of Audrey the hairdresser, played by Sue Nicholls. She had been a character in *Corrie* for over twenty-five years. It wasn't a huge part, but it was quite fun.

I remember ringing my agent before travelling up to Manchester and saying, 'Do you think I ought to try a northern accent? I've done them when I've been recording audio books but I didn't feel very comfortable pretending to be northern when it isn't something I do well, and all of them speak with a very strong northern accent.' He said, 'Well it's one of those difficult things. If they've offered it to you, then obviously they're not really expecting a northern accent, but if you want to be considered as a long-term character then maybe you should try just a slight one.'

So I went up on the train and obviously there is no rehearsal time for a series like *Corrie*. It's straight in with no background knowledge of your character. You're very lucky if you meet the people you're doing your scene with beforehand, then you have two quick camera run-throughs and that's it. It's instant acting – something I hadn't done for a very long time. I was used to theatre and long rehearsals, getting to know the cast and everyone working together to the same end, with a director who actually directs you.

The prospect of walking in to do these few scenes was quite scary. Nigel Havers was acting with me in my storyline and I knew him a bit, but I didn't know Sue Nicholls, I didn't know the director and, as I say, I didn't know the *Corrie* story very well. I'd been for a shopping expedition with the costume guy, Lance, about a week beforehand. I arrived in Manchester and went to my hotel overnight, then straight in first thing in the morning and into hairdressing and make-up – it's a bit like a private club. There are some people who had been in this series for forty or fifty years, others for twenty-five years, and then there's a whole younger contingent, some of whom have been in it since they were eleven and are now in their early twenties. So everyone knows everyone else really well and it's like walking into a club or a family. You feel you're joining something but as a newbie you also feel very isolated.

Luckily Sue and I hit it off and I managed to find a little bit of time in the green room to discuss with her what sort of relationship we had and how long we thought it might have been going on for. And then I said to her, 'Look, Sue, be honest with me, do you think I ought to try and put on a slight northern accent?'

In our first scene together, we are both coming out of the ladies' toilets at some big function and my first line was 'The cleanliness in these toilets is second to none', which is not exactly a line you think of as everyday conversation – also it's quite a difficult sentence to say.

She said, 'Well, how do you feel about it?' and I answered, 'Not very confident to be honest, regional accents are not my forte.'

'Try it out on me.'

'The cleanliness in these toilets is second to none...'

'Take it down a bit, and try and push your voice off a bit.'

So I tried again: 'The cleanliness in these toilets is second to none...'

'No, don't bother.'

Then there were a couple of fairly decent scenes with Nigel Havers's character Lewis Archer, who had come with me as my boyfriend, though it was clear from the moment he and Audrey set eyes on each other that there was a sort of spark between the two of them.

She didn't know at the time I had got Lewis from an escort agency. She was surprised that I, more or less the same age as her, had suddenly managed to pull this rather dashing lothario.

At the end of the episode, I slipped her a card with the name of the escort agency and said, 'You know, if you're interested, why don't you ring them up?'

As for me, an actress getting into the part, I knew I was her 'posh' friend, a fairly successful hairdresser with a salon that was upmarket compared to Audrey's. I didn't need to learn how to be a hairdresser to play Claudia, but as it happens I'd studied hairdressing anyway. I've always done all the family's hair and I used to cut various friends' hair too – I'm good with hair.

I ended up not doing a northern accent as such but just trying to flatten the vowels a tiny bit. Then we got into actually doing the first scene – my baptism by fire. Of course I'd rehearsed my lines and knew them back to front and inside out, but I wasn't prepared for the speed at which they do these things. On previous television jobs, which weren't serials like this, there were three or four takes until you felt happy, and the director too. This was one take – fine, great and on to the next one. You didn't have the luxury of saying, 'Uh, I'd really like to do that again.'

Though I hadn't worked with him before, I had met Nigel socially so I felt there was a connection. He's a very easy and generous actor anyway and the script had Claudia and Audrey instantly getting into the sort of banter you'd expect from two middle-aged women who had obviously known each other well but had a sort of love–hate relationship.

Sue and I clicked almost instantaneously, not just as the characters but also in real life. And at the end of that day, the director said, 'It was really great. You pulled something out of that which wasn't on the page.'

Very soon there were more episodes offered. It was never a solid run, but five or six episodes, then a bit of a gap and then four or five. In all, I did about twenty-five over the period of a year. And they did develop the character and I had some really smashing scenes with Sue, which focused more on their love–hate bitching but also revealed some loving kindness in the relationship.

There was a very funny storyline that came in after Nigel had gone. I was treating Audrey to a hairstyle at my place and a very good-looking gentleman turned up. Again, he was supposedly a beau of mine and again, Audrey apparently fell in love with him. He turned out to be a transvestite.

For the first few times I was still very nervous; I was still a stranger. It wasn't just the speed but the fact that they have three or four episodes on the go at the same time with different directors. There was an awful lot of hanging around – there always is – and huge yawning gaps in the middle of the day when there was nothing to do. And of course, the paparazzi and the public hang around the gated area outside the *Corrie* set and whenever they see a new face they start taking photographs and speculating about what might be happening.

When there were breaks, and people were not in their dressing rooms, they would be sitting reading or looking at scripts or eating their lunch or doing a crossword puzzle or signing their autographs and so on – and everyone was extremely welcoming and easy-going. In a very short time, I felt part of that community. But, because most of the regulars in *Corrie* have been in it for years and years and they all live in the area, or not very far away, there wasn't a social life when the day finished as there is in the theatre. They would go home to their families or their partners.

So when I was there for four or five days on the trot – and I managed to do a deal with one of the little boutique hotels in Manchester, so I was extremely comfortable – there was no life when the working day or the night shoot finished, and I found it a bit lonely in the evenings. There are only so many times when you feel like going out to the cinema on your own or going to the shops in Piccadilly. But actually doing the series was great fun.

I would always know my lines inside out before coming on the set because that was what I was used to, but quite often I would see people (because the shots were quite short) swotting up on just two or three lines. Then they'd do them from lots of different angles. But later on in my storyline there were three or four sizeable scenes with quite a long emotional journey so I enjoyed doing my homework beforehand and knowing exactly how I was going to play it without an awful lot of help, because there just wasn't time for direction and experimentation.

There was a lot of public approval of the relationship that

had been developed between Audrey and Claudia, our two characters. I really thought that this had a lot of mileage and I was hoping that it would continue. So when the episodes that I'd been given finished, I said to my agent that I would love to do more if there was a decent storyline proposed. But so far it hasn't happened. Claudia isn't dead, she just stormed off in high dudgeon. She could return.

There was quite a lot of interest in the press about Rula Lenska in *Coronation Street*. It surprised them as it had surprised me when it was first suggested. But then all manner of people have been in the *Street*, from Ian McKellen to Prince Charles. Everybody loves *Coronation Street* and so do I.

Being on it was like *Celebrity Big Brother*. Once it started airing, wodges of fan mail arrived and I was being stopped in the street. Even a couple of years on, people came up to me in the street and said, 'When is Claudia coming back? Come on, they can't stop it like that. I thought it was such a wonderful relationship.' It was great fun. If someone had said to me, 'What's the least likely job you think you would ever be offered?' *Coronation Street* would have been near the top of the list. I'm very proud to have been part of something people love so much. And as happens quite often when I have really enjoyed myself, I felt prompted to break into verse:

It's truly an honour to be on the *Street*
And part of the Weatherfield crowd…

A dream unexpected that really came true,

Of which I will always be proud.

This Manchester miracle with fifty years' fame

Is the best of the best in the soap opera game.

The scripts are great and the actors are grand,

There's a feeling of family in dear *Corrie* Land!

And instant acting for me was so new,

Switching on Claudia from the single word CUE!

I have learned such a lot and will miss one and all

So a huge great big thank you, it's just been a ball

Old Claudia salutes with all of her heart.

It was such a delight that you gave her this part,

There are few pleasures greater than sparring with Aud

When she raises her scissors to lacerate Claud

Adieu … Farewell … what a wonderful time

Corrie, fifty years old and still in her prime

I was travelling either to or from Manchester to do *Coronation Street* when I got a phone call from my daughter. I was on a crowded train and I could hear her in tears on the other end of the phone saying, 'He's done it. He's done it. He's done it.' I kept saying, 'Done what? I can't really talk because I'm on a crowded train.' And finally, through her tears she burst out, 'He's asked me to marry him.' Lara had been with her boyfriend for a couple of years – he's a really nice, loyal, stalwart, great friend, and he was by far my favourite boyfriend she'd ever had. They had been sharing a flat in Richmond together. Lara was a trained paediatric nurse, working at Great Ormond Street Hospital, a wonderful nurse who certainly has a vocation for looking after children. She's very patient, very warm and very loving – and children absolutely adore her.

So we started planning for the wedding, which of course brought her father Brian's family together, though sadly both sets of grandparents were no longer with us. We chose a Church of England church in Richmond and had the reception at Ham Polo Club. It was an absolutely beautiful day, full of friends and relatives, about 120 in all, with beautiful speeches and dancing.

Towards the end of the evening, quite a lot of champagne having been consumed, the whole of the Polish contingent got together to dance and sing 'We Are Family' over and over and over again. Brian and I had paid for a honeymoon suite in a hotel in Richmond for the couple, and after that they set off to Mauritius for their honeymoon.

When one's only child gets married, you feel an enormous sense of achievement and a great feeling of satisfaction and peace. Lara has chosen a really good person. I think in the beginning he and his family may have been a little taken aback by this tumult of Poles, particularly at the wedding, because I imagine we are slightly scary when we are all together, but I think he's got used to it. Lara is definitely more sensible than I am. She doesn't have the same wanderlust or need for adventure, discovery and travel. She's very much a homebody and so is he.

Within a couple of years of them being married I got the joyous news that they were expecting their first child. I was told in no uncertain terms by both of them that I was not to rush over to the West Middlesex Hospital as soon as I knew the baby had arrived. I had to wait until I was summoned. And of course, typical me, I couldn't. Within a couple of hours I was charging over there. I have been very much a hands-on grandmother. Lara had a difficult pregnancy so I took time off work then and certainly for the first six months of the little boy's life, and I have never experienced a greater joy and thrill. I still get it now and hope it will continue for many years to come.

Of course there's a danger of grandmother interfering and saying, 'Are you sure you should be doing that, and isn't it a bit too early? And isn't that a bit too much?' I really hope I have learnt not to do that. Brian, who always has been a wonderful father to Lara, is now a wonderful grandfather and we regularly have family lunches at my house and get-togethers for birthdays and Christmases. My grandson is a great unifier.

CHAPTER 26

FROM PRINCE PHILIP TO MICHAEL WINNER

When I was younger, I was occasionally told I looked a little bit like Rita Hayworth. I certainly had similar hair but, actually, if you look back at photographs of me at that time, in certain lights, in profile, with the hair falling right over one side of my face, I looked more like Veronica Lake than Rita Hayworth.

At the Royal Variety Performance of 1985 some of us were invited to become screen goddesses. Gloria Hunniford was Doris Day, Stephanie Lawrence, fabulous but sadly no longer with us, was Marilyn Monroe and I was Rita Hayworth – Hayworth as Gilda singing 'Put the Blame on Mame' at the Royal Variety Performance. How wonderful! How scary!

I was sent off for fittings for a facsimile of the amazing dress that Hayworth wore as Gilda in 1946, a beautiful black fitted number, sleeveless, with an enormous bow at the back. I had long gloves, of course. The hair was all my own. But I was busy working on something else so the fittings were rather few and far between and they got the size of the dress one size smaller than it should have been, particularly in the bosom (of which I haven't got very much).

I was terrified of singing and I had to do this enormous number and be a siren. Hayworth said her tragedy was that 'men go to bed with Gilda and wake up with me'. I just wanted to be Hayworth for a couple of minutes. It wasn't made easier by this strapless dress being a size too small. I was very conscious that if I put my arms down at all, whatever spare flesh there was seemed to bubble over the top.

At the same Variety Performance Dennis was doing 'We're a Couple of Swells' with Maureen Lipman. I remember her saying she was constantly trying to chase him to rehearse in the wings and he was always out at the pub until the last minute.

Once the curtain had come down we all lined up to meet the Queen and the Duke of Edinburgh. Dame Anna Neagle was next to me on my left, and right up at the top of the line was Joan Collins – and I remember thinking that was slightly wrong. Surely Dame Anna Neagle should have had pride of place. Anyway, the Queen set off well ahead of the Duke of Edinburgh, who, with his hands traditionally clasped behind his back, stopped and was having quite a nice conversation with Gloria Hunniford, Stephanie Lawrence and me. He was saying that Rita Hayworth was one of his favourite actresses from the forties when suddenly we heard a rather distinct 'Philip!' It was the Queen. He bowed hurriedly to the three of us, kissed us all on the hand and hurried off to join Her Majesty.

✻

Being in the business, I have met a lot of very famous people. 'Do you ever get tongue-tied when you meet someone who's a real hero of yours?' I've often been asked. The answer is 'not often', but there are exceptions.

Dennis and I were at the summer party David Frost and his wife Carina throw each year in Chelsea, a very glamorous affair packed with glitterati from politics, show business, sport and sundry other worlds. We were standing in a small group talking with Sean Connery, who has always been a heart-throb of mine, and the remarkable Zsa Zsa Gabor, when suddenly on the other side of this crowded tent I saw Sidney Poitier.

I imagine I let out a gasp, then I said to Dennis, 'Oh my God, I can't believe it, Sidney Poitier,' and Zsa Zsa Gabor caught me by the arm and said, 'Darlink, you like him?' I said, 'Oh, he's been an idol of mine for as long as I can remember … *In the Heat of the Night.*' And she said, 'No problem, darlink, I know him very well.' So she grabbed me by the arm and propelled me through the crowd and just sort of pushed me in front of Sidney Poitier. I was completely dumbstruck.

I wanted to say something intelligent about how wonderful an actor he was and how I'd followed his career and I loved the parts that he'd played, and particularly *In the Heat of the Night*, but I was completely unable to utter a word. I just about managed, 'Uh, ah, uh, ah,' holding my hands out in front of me. I remember he put his hands on either side of my hands, looked deep into my eyes and said, 'Miss Lenska, it's such a privilege to meet you.' Guess who's not coming to dinner!

❧

I first made the acquaintance of hot-air balloons at charity fund-raising events for Children with Leukaemia. At the start it was just photo opportunities, with the balloon never really taking off. They were tethered so they were just a little off the ground. I had a terrible fear of flying in those days. I used to have to be dosed up to the eyeballs before setting foot on a plane.

These appearances proved very popular and they did raise a lot of money for Children with Leukaemia, or the Paul O'Gorman Foundation as it was then called. Then Flying Pictures, the company with whom I did these photographs in the balloon, suggested maybe it would be a good idea if I trained to be a pilot. I used to fly a balloon sponsored by Alka-Seltzer. It said on the side 'Plink, plink, fizz'.

Training to be a hot-air-balloon pilot is just like going for a fixed-wing licence: you have to do Farmer's Union Laws, you have to understand some meteorology, you have to do all the mathematics about ambient air temperature and the weight of the people in the basket and wind speed etc. Quite complicated. Anyway, I had a couple of very good instructors and I did finally pass my pilot's licence, although I must admit I've never actually flown solo. There's always been an experienced pilot with me.

We flew all over the country – probably most glamorously from Leeds Castle, where I once ballooned with Per Lindstrand and Sir Richard Branson.

Later, when we were living out in Buckinghamshire, a lot of the flying used to be from Great Missenden and of course the kids absolutely loved it, as did Dennis to a certain extent. Once, when in Africa, we flew over the Masai Mara, which was incredible. After that, flying over the English countryside, where the most interesting wildlife you ever saw was pigs, horses or cows, rather lost its charm so I stopped. To keep your pilot's licence up you have to do a certain number of hours a year. Within about two years I was not reaching my quota, so I'm officially an ex-pilot.

On one occasion we landed in the grounds at Gatcombe Park and met Princess Anne. I asked her, 'Would you like to come up with me in the balloon, Ma'am?' And she said, 'You know, I've always wanted to do that, but I don't think Mummy would like it.' That's her excuse for not ballooning. I haven't got one.

✣

My first interview for a film part was with Michael Winner. It was a horror movie, and it was a horror interview too. Only recently out of drama school, I was summoned to meet him at his offices, somewhere in town.

I was running late and I was wearing skintight, white Lycra trousers – this was in the summer. My hair was very long then and I was in the back of a cab, desperately trying to put on my make-up. We went over a bump and my foundation spilt in my lap. All over my crotch and my tummy there were very unattractive dark brown stains and the top that I was wearing wasn't long enough to cover them.

What do I do? What do I do? Then I had this brilliant idea. I would take the trousers off and put them on back to front but I'd have to be careful how I walked – I'd have to enter Winner's office without ever showing him my back.

I arrived at his office and was told to sit in the waiting room. I was feeling extremely self-conscious. Then I got the call. The door to his office was ajar. I was standing in the doorway and he was sitting at his big desk, with his feet up and a big cigar jammed in his mouth, talking to someone on the phone. He didn't really acknowledge me so I just stood there with my portfolio (in those days, you used to carry photographs of the different things you'd been in).

I must have waited for about five minutes. Finally he put

the phone down, didn't move his feet or his cigar, and said, 'Are you going to stand there all day?' I said, 'Oh, sorry, Mr Winner.' I went in, sat down and passed over my portfolio and he had a quick look through it. 'You're a good-looking girl, aren't you?'

'Thank you, Mr Winner.'

He said, 'Is that a wig you're wearing?' And I said, 'No, it's my own hair.'

'Well it looks like a fucking wig!'

Then he asked for my vital statistics, so I told him and we chatted a little longer about this and that. Then it was clear the interview was over. So I got up and backed towards the door with him looking at me as if I was completely stupid. His last words were 'Let's face it, your tits aren't big enough for horror movies!'

❦

I met Martina Navratilova through animal charities. I was working with Tusk and Wildlife Line and she came over to play the Honda Challenge Tennis at the Albert Hall. There was a press conference afterwards and I asked her, 'Martina, what is more important to you? Putting Czechoslovakia on the map, or being the greatest female tennis player the world has ever known?' And she said, 'That's a very interesting and intelligent question.' And we just got on.

After that, every time she came over to England, either to play or to commentate at Wimbledon, she would invite me. On a couple of occasions when she was over for Sports Personality of the Year or various public functions and her partner either hadn't come over with her from the States or didn't want to accompany her, she would ring and ask me to join her.

On the first couple of occasions when we were seen together on television or at Wimbledon's Centre Court, I would get texts from people asking, 'Is there something we should know between you and Martina?' I had to disappoint them. I'm not as much in contact with her now as I used to be, but she's been a good friend.

I was with her, watching on Centre Court a few years ago, and during a break I went to the loo and, as I was coming back, there was Margaret Thatcher coming down the stairs, supported on either side by two young ladies who worked at Wimbledon, and I couldn't stop myself. I went up to her, curt-sied and said, 'Lady Thatcher, it's such an enormous honour to meet you.' And she looked at me and said, 'I thought you played extremely well my dear!'

CHAPTER 27

HOPE YOU ENJOYED THE SHOW

How does one end a book about a life that is, I hope, nowhere near its end? I remember my mother often saying to me how, as one gets older, life seems to speed past ever more quickly. As with many other things she said, I didn't believe her, but it is so true. I am amazed at how time has flown recently. Though my life has been a rich and full tapestry so far, I feel there is so much left to do, experience and achieve.

Some things get easier with age, like not caring quite so much what people think of you. I have certainly learnt that you cannot be responsible for other people's reactions. I am who I am and if that doesn't please certain people, that's their problem, not mine. I honestly do not regret anything I have done in my life apart from when I have caused pain and hardship to others.

My mother was a matriarch par excellence, a mantle that should have passed to me as the eldest. All three of us daughters have so much of her in our make-up and though I have sometimes been the main organiser, it is definitely my youngest sister Anna who has inherited Mama's unconditional caring nature, always being there for all her friends and family – one of life's truly unselfish pearls.

Perhaps life would have been simpler and easier had I lived in the middle lane, but then I would not have experienced the extreme highs and excitements that I have, though of course I quite often have had to pay the price in the extreme lows that followed. But not one single moment of my life has been boring.

Sometimes I have dived in, following my instinct and my heart when I should have allowed my head and my brain to have more of an influence. Despite my Mama's advice I always thought this was the only way to live and that I was being true to myself.

I never imagined the untold joy and thrill of becoming a grandmother. This new little person in my world, this little grandson, the child of my beloved only daughter, brings boundless joy and another reason for living.

I hope with all my heart that plenty of worthwhile work and challenges lie ahead and perhaps a love to share this final third of my life, but I also know I am surrounded and embraced by my precious daughter and her family, my very special siblings and closest friends. From my mother I learnt the vital importance of family and girlfriends.

I still yearn for adventure – and sometimes danger – and

the constant proof to myself that I am needed and useful. Sometimes the body seems not as able as it once was but the spirit is constantly willing.

PICTURE CREDITS

I would like to thank Brian Aris for his very kind donation of images to the book, and also Nick Dawkes, for the front cover.

Plate section 1, p. 2, bottom right © Press Association

p. 182 © Andy Huntley

All other images reproduced are from my personal collection.